READING TAROT CARDS

A Guide to The New Palladini Tarot

READING TAROT CARDS

A Guide to

T H E
NEW PALLADINI
T A R O T

Susan Hansson

Publisher
U.S. GAMES SYSTEMS, INC.
Stamford, CT USA

First Edition

Hansson, Susan.
 Reading Tarot Cards:
 A Guide to The New Palladini Tarot.

Library of Congress Catalog Card Number: 96-061383

ISBN: 0-88079-997-8

10 9 8 7 6 5 4 3 2

Printed in Canada

U.S. GAMES SYSTEMS, INC.
179 Ludlow Street
Stamford, CT 06902 USA

THIS BOOK IS DEDICATED WITH LOVE AND DEVOTION

to my husband Richard
and precious children
Adam, Richie, and Lauren.

MY SINCERE THANKS AND APPRECIATION

to Richard Hansson,
Janice Doherty,
Jeanne Gerulskis,
Irene Tewksbury,
and Mark Sullivan for help
in editing the manuscript.

SPECIAL THANKS

to Janice Doherty
for the illustration
of the Tree of Life.

TABLE OF CONTENTS

INTRODUCTION

The origins of the Tarot are unknown, which adds to the charm and beauty of the mysterious deck of cards. They have been linked to the ancient Egyptians where pictures similar to the 22 Major Arcana were found on the walls of an initiation path in the lower chambers of the Sphinx. They have been connected to ancient India, since the androgynous Hindu god Ardhanari holds in its arms four objects similar to the four suits of the Tarot. They have been traced to Fez, Morocco and Ancient Greece. Antoine Court de Gebelin wrote in 1781 that the Tarot was actually a book saved from fires in the ancient Egyptian temples. He believed they contained the wisdom transcribed in The Book of Thoth. Thoth was the Lord of Magic who is often depicted with the body of a man and the head and neck of an ibis. He is often drawn holding a writing instrument, tablet, and palm branch. The Greeks gave Thoth the name Hermes Trismegistus and referred to his secret work as Hermetic. The Tarot has also been linked to ancient Hebrew wisdom in the Cabalah, which will be outlined in this book.

Tarot cards received much attention in Italy in the 15th century. Beautiful decks were created, including one for the Visconti family, which survived. Some of these decks are in a private collection of the Pierpont Morgan Library,

New York. The three volumes of *The Encyclopedia of Tarot* by Stuart R. Kaplan hold thousands of carefully documented Tarot cards interpreted throughout the ages in all manner of styles. The cards have fascinated artists and captivated the interest of people throughout the ages despite eras of religious opposition. In 1378, all card playing was banned in Regensburg, Germany. Somewhere between 1470-90, a Franciscan friar banned the 22 cards of the Major Arcana in Italy. Gypsies, who traveled extensively and are well-known for fortune telling with cards, were given the credit for spreading them throughout Northern Europe.

The Hermetic Order of the Golden Dawn began around the turn of the 20th century and clarified the meanings of Tarot cards by using illustrative symbolism, including astrology, color, numerology, the Hebrew alphabet, Jewish and Christian mysticism, alchemy, myths, and folklore. Their members' books are still in print and their teachings are inspirational and profound.

The New Palladini Tarot deck by David Palladini was created with rich, vivid colors and classical imagery from the extensive studies of the Golden Dawn. He utilizes timeless archetypal symbols from religions, myths, folklore, and history. The artist's unique work and excellence in design capture the true spirit and magic that make each Tarot card's meaning come alive. The beginning of this book explains the structure and components that make up the Tarot. The middle section shows each of the 78 New Palladini Tarot cards, a description, and classic divinatory meaning. Since the classic interpretations date back to the turn of the 20th century and earlier, I have also included updated interpretations. The last section explains and illustrates several different card spreads, shows sample interpretations, and offers tips to help you work with the cards.

STRUCTURE
OF THE TAROT

A standard Tarot deck consists of 78 cards which are divided into two groups. The 22 cards of the Major Arcana or "secrets" are the most powerful since they contain the imagery of spiritual and major life issues and help decipher fate and destiny. The famous psychoanalyst, Carl G. Jung, wrote that the Major Arcana symbols are related to the archetypes of the collective unconscious. Archetypes are patterns and original models that translate into pictures. Analyzing the pictures trigger thoughts and emotions that can help us understand ourselves. For example, throughout the ages the sun has been understood to symbolize warmth and God's love, energy, happiness, and glory. The image and connotation is imprinted in our minds. The symbols of the Tarot evoke these memories, and that is part of their "magic." Intuition and perception are helpful to read cards and these traits are exercised and developed through continued use of the Tarot.

MAJOR ARCANA

The 22 Major Arcana or "secrets" are divided into three septenaries, plus the Fool.

1 - 7 The Magician, The High Priestess, The Empress, The Emperor, The Hierophant, The Lovers, and The Chariot
The cards represent the collective traits and qualities personified in the forces of the dynamic psyche.

8 - 14 Strength, The Hermit, The Wheel of Fortune, Justice, The Hanged Man, Death, and Temperance
These represent spiritual influence on the soul. They are affected by the ways and laws of cause and effect.

15 - 21 The Devil, The Tower, The Star, The Moon, The Sun, The Last Judgement, and The World
These cards are higher, more complex, but more pure and basic forces of existence.

0 The Fool
This card can be placed at the beginning or end of the deck. He is in a position of infinite energy. I place him at the beginning since he reminds me of whirling energy before manifestation of action. He is also placed at the beginning of the New Palladini Tarot.

MINOR ARCANA

The Minor Arcana consist of 56 cards that have been related to the modern 52-card playing deck, with the addition of four Knights and four Pages rather than the playing card deck's four Jacks. The Minor Arcana is divided into four suits: Swords, Rods, Cups, and Pentacles. They refer to events, people, places, and things in everyday life. The court cards consist of Kings and Queens who represent people, and Knights and Pages who represent both people and the coming and going of matters. The suit's attributes are described in the section of the Minor Arcana. The suits, numerology, astrology, color psychology, and the Cabalah are all incorporated into the Major and Minor Arcana.

SWORDS

Swords symbolize the formative world of expression. They are illustrated as long, sharp swords similar to the ones forged in the days of knights in armor. The swords' powerful image is phallic and masculine. They represent aggression, the courageous pursuit of justice and power, strong ideas, action, forcefulness, alertness, assertion, extroverted thinking, and cold detachment of thought from emotion. They can also be abstract and clinical. The negative attributes include blind ambition, destruction, suffering, hatred, and war. They are related to the suit of spades in the modern 52-card deck of playing cards.

Element: Air

Season: Winter

Astrological Correspondents: Gemini, Libra, Aquarius

General Characteristics: Intellect, justice, balance. Observations, perceptions, opinions. Courage, determination, force. Restlessness, change. Socially oriented, diplomatic. Rebellious, indecisive, distant, vague.

RODS

Rods represent the archetypal world of pure ideas. They are drawn as clubs with growing leaves and flowers. They are connected to intellect, growth, energy, will, inspiration, determination, strength, and force. They represent nature, agriculture and creation. The buds, leaves, and flowers symbolize change, growth, and renewal. They are sometimes referred to as wands or staves and are related to the suit of clubs in modern playing cards.

Element: Fire

Season: Autumn

Astrological Correspondents: Aries, Leo, Sagittarius

General Characteristics: Energy, assertiveness, force of action to create change and promote growth. In a reading, the rods refer to these qualities and the strength of will to change ideas into actions. Inspired, aggressive, extroverted, masculine energy.

Cups

The cups represent the creative world of human emotions. They are drawn as elegant gold chalices of a sacred nature. Cups hold the liquid that is the very essence of the human soul. They symbolize love, happiness, the human spirit. Cups, being containers, are connected to the feminine principle, sensitive and nurturing. Love, marriage, feelings. They are considered lucky in a reading and are related to hearts in the modern 52-card pack.

Element: Water

Season: Summer

Astrological Correspondents: Pisces, Cancer, Scorpio

General Characteristics: Mothering, nurturing, home-loving, and family-oriented. Fertility, strong endurance, passion, intensity, dependency. Romance, marriages, births. Serene, sensitive, receptive, insightful, prophetic, mystical. Purifying, self-sacrificing, martyr.

Pentacles

Pentacles (or coins) represent the material world and its concerns. They are drawn as a five-pointed star (pentagram) within a circle. The pentagram is a symbol of magical arts, the five senses of man, the five elements of nature, and the five extremities of the human body. The circle around the pentagram represents the world, the kingdom, the continuity of life. DaVinci's famous illustration of man as the microcosm within the macrocosm is a man drawn within a circle with a pentagram connecting the five extremities. Pentacles are related to diamonds in the modern 52-card pack.

Element: Earth

Season: Spring

Astrological Correspondents: Taurus, Virgo, Capricorn

General Characteristics: Earthly, stable. Material concerns, finances, work, business, trade, development, barter. In a reading, the appearance of many pentacle cards indicates wealth and material interests. Stubborn, intelligent, physical.

COLOR

Colors evoke certain responses. The symbolism of various colors are listed below:

YELLOW—The color of the sun evokes happiness, warmth, spiritual blessing, divine inspiration, divine intervention.

BLUE—Peace, purity, gentleness. Pure water, reality, tranquillity. Distance, infinity. Blue skies. Pleasure.

WHITE—Light, purity, innocence.

BLACK—Darkness, evil, death. Sadness, depression.

GOLD—Godliness, divine justice, divine word. Riches, glory.

RED—Passion, physical love, aggression, dynamism, anger, blood.

GREEN—Hope, wisdom in action, love of nature, nature's cycles, springtime, renewal.

NUMEROLOGY

Numerology is the science of numbers. The Cabalists connected letters representing sound and vibrational patterns with numeral identities. Each number and letter has a sacred meaning. This system is related to the Vedic system of India and to Chaldean numerology.

ONE—Alpha. Singularity. Individuality. Success through one's own efforts. A leader, pioneering type. An accomplished, respected person. Essence. Beginnings.
Negative aspect: Self-centered.

TWO—Balance of opposites. Wisdom. A good companion, harmonious and diplomatic. Psychic, intuitive, sensitive to feelings of others. Patience. A good mediator. Partnerships.
Negative aspects: Broken agreements, duality.

THREE—Productive. Creative. Ability to inspire and incite others. Expressive. Good temperament. Sociable. Organizer. Success in the arts and communication fields.
Negative aspects: Poor communications, over-indulgence.

FOUR—Stability. Measurement. Logic. Success in math, sciences, architecture, building. Analytical and systematic. Honest, hardworking, dependable.
Negative aspects: Mundane, slow, unimaginative.

FIVE—Changeable. A life of action and flurry of events. Need to harness and find a vehicle for unbounded energy whether it be religion, politics, or creative projects.
Negative aspects: Conflicts and confusion.

SIX—Love. Beauty. Harmony. Perfection. Love of family and home life. Ability to create beautiful interiors and exteriors. Collections. An inspirational person. Fair-minded and helpful.
Negative aspects: Martyrdom, angst.

SEVEN—Safety. Security. Intuition. Deep thought. Engineering ability. Arts and sciences. A lucky person. Healer. Sensitive. Need to specialize and work hard on relationships.
Negative aspects: Scattered energy, superficiality.

EIGHT—Justice. Individuality. Rhythm and balance. Worldly success. Ability to generate wealth. Often misunderstood to be cold when actually very deep and intense. Believer in commitments and honor. Failures only intensify struggle for success. Fair and merciful.
Negative aspects: Out of balance, instability.

NINE—Attainment. Fulfillment. Completion. Contentment. Pursuit of pleasure in work, social life, and home. Mystical, magical number. Protective. Possessive. Humanitarian, spiritual type. Tendency to dwell on losses too much. Worrier. People feel comfortable around this type.
Negative aspects: Worrier, extremist, possible emotional problems.

CABALAH

The Cabalah is an ancient theosophy based upon esoteric meanings of the Hebrew Scriptures. The Cabalists hid their wisdom in an intricate system of numbers and letters. The system's beliefs are based in the letters IHVH, which stand for "That Which Is, That Which Shall Be." The four letters are broken down into four worlds which relate to the Tarot:

The Formative World of expression, connected to the suit of Swords.

The Archetypal World of pure ideas, connected to the suit of Rods.

The Creative World and the patterning of ideas, connected to the suit of Cups.

The Material World of physical objects, connected to the suit of Pentacles.

Cabalist philosophy is illustrated in the Tree of Life, which is a system of arranging various levels of consciousness and spiritual development reached at each of ten Sephiroth (stages). The 22 paths of the Tree of Life start at Kether, which is the Godhead of Limitless Light, and descend down the tree to Malkuth, the physical world. The 22 paths from the Godhead to the physical world have been related to the 22 Major Arcana and start with the pure, whirling, blissful energy of the Fool. Each Major Arcana archetype describes characteristics, lessons, and challenges of the paths as they descend to the last path, 22, The World, which leads to Malkuth, the physical world. The human spirit is thought to have descended these paths from Limitless light and now must attempt to ascend to reunite. The diagram shows each Sephiroth and the 22 paths. There is a Tarot spread (pp. 212-214) using the Tree of Life in the chapter on readings.

The Tree of Life

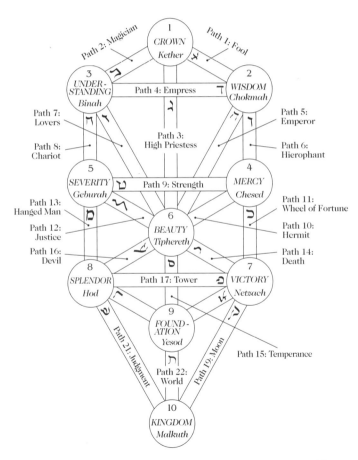

The letters are charted as follows:

Hebrew Letter	Meaning	Tarot Correspondent
Aleph	bull, ox	The Fool
Beth	house	The Magician
Gimel	camel	The High Priestess
Daleth	womb	The Empress
Heh	window	The Emperor
Vav	nail, hook	The Hierophant
Zayin	sword, weapon	The Lovers
Cheth	fence	The Chariot
Teth	snake	Strength
Yod	open hand	The Hermit
Kaph	closed hand	The Wheel of Fortune
Lamed	ox goad	Justice
Mem	water	The Hanged Man
Nun	fish	Death
Samekh	tent peg	Temperance
Ayin	eye, anger	The Devil
Pe	mouth	The Tower
Tzaddi	fish hook	The Star
Qoph	head	The Moon
Resh	head and face	The Sun
Shin	tooth	The Last Judgement
Tav	mark	The World

THE MAJOR ARCANA

THE FOOL

THE FOOL

Key 0

Numeral 0: Infinite, pure energy in perpetual motion.

Hebrew Letter: Aleph: air, bull, ox, man. Air is the vehicle for communication.

Cabalah: Path 1: Kether (God) to Hokmah (father).

Astrological Influence: Uranus. The planet known as "the awakener," it has great potential to be constructive or destructive. Uranus is erratic and unpredictable; it stimulates ideas, change, and freedom.

THE FOOL CAN BE PLACED AT THE BEGINNING OR the end of the Major Arcana. He represents the state of grace and purity of energy at the ascent and descent from the Godhead. Guided by intuition and precognition, he is oblivious to the mundane concerns of everyday life. Dressed in the blissful colors of the heavens, he resembles Siddhartha, the young prince who fled the security of the palace walls to experience the world. He eventually returns to become the understanding and compassionate king who evolved to become Buddha. The Fool of the Tarot also journeys alone through the social boundaries of man with an open mind. In his hand he carries a flower as pure and white as his motivation. Over his shoulder he carries the rod of spirit, intuition, and fire. The handle is brilliant gold, touched by the power, energy, and light of the sun, which glows in the background. He proceeds optimistically, oblivious to impending dangers, emphasized by his position on a cliff's edge. Like the medieval jester, he wanders with the same good-natured ease into the king's castle as into the peasant's village.

The ancients believed fools were linked directly to God. Christians believed madmen had a clearer idea of Spirit since they were so removed from society and therefore not bogged down by the material, physical pursuits of man. The Tarot's Fool will wander into your life, inspire you, and then, like the wind, he will move on. Remember, although he has descended straight from the Limitless Light, he is now tainted by the earthly plane and can use his disarming innocence for tricky, indifferent, crazy, even lawless behavior.

Classic Divinatory Meaning: Boundless energy. Beginning a new growth cycle. Potential. Choice of several paths available. Youthfulness. A new journey.

Reversed: Wrong choices, bad decisions. Madness. Folly and foolhardy behavior.

Modern Meaning: Young at heart. Blissful enthusiasm in beginning a new venture. Recycling old ideas. Plans with new insights. Tremendous potential. Instinct pushes one to gather up all the thoughts and ideas and pursue them regardless of hindrances. Beginning to ascend or descend into a powerful new phase.

Reversed: Irresponsible thinking. Reckless, even disastrous, behavior. Foolish impulses.

THE MAGICIAN

Key 1

Numeral 1: Singularity. The uniqueness of the individual. The human soul.

Hebrew Letter: Beth: house. That which houses the soul of man.

Cabalah: Path 2: Kether (God) to Binah (mother).

Astrological Influence: Mercury. The planet of the instinctive mind, intelligence, speed, magic, dexterity, and thoughts. The messenger.

THE MAGICIAN IS THE WILL PERSONIFIED. HE IS THE dwelling place for the Spirit in man. He is the ego and will, trained to manipulate his environment to attain his own ends. He is active and sexually potent. The ouroboros snake devours its own tail around his waist to symbolize continuity. The cosmic lemniscate above his head means harmony, eternal life, and dominion. He has keen concentration and powers of transformation which can make things happen or appear to happen. He can be the illusionist who performs and transforms with perfect synchronicity and seemingly magical ease. His right hand points to the heavens as the source of his power. His left hand points to earth and below. The Magician is situated halfway between good and evil with the potential for both.

THE MAGICIAN

He has learned the secrets of the four suits which are set upon the table before him: Cup (water), Rod (fire), Sword (air), and Pentacle (earth). Like the alchemists of the Hermetic order, he seeks to create, control, and transform. The alchemists used the symbol of the metal mercury for the dwelling place of the Divine. In the Tarot, the Magician is the dwelling place of the Divine. In oriental philosophy, he represents the masculine, creative principle of the Godhead known as yang.

Classic Divinatory Meaning: Will, skill, concentration, and desire. Original thinker. A powerful person, adept and capable.

Reversed: Trickery and deceit. Selfishness. Chicanery.

Modern Meaning: Strong-willed, intelligent, goal-oriented person. Dexterous and proficient. The ability to concentrate and manipulate people and situations to achieve goals. Self-motivated, confident, healthy ego. Careful planning and alignment ensure achievement. A capable person with almost hypnotic powers of persuasion. Active yang principle.

Reversed: A con artist. Selfish person. Self-gratification. A crafty person who takes advantage of weaker types. A user. Empty promises from a very skillful manipulator.

THE HIGH PRIESTESS

THE HIGH PRIESTESS

Key 2

Numeral 2: Knowledge. Holding Pattern. Gentle, passive, artistic.

Hebrew Letter: Gimel: wisdom. The holding place of knowledge as yet unrevealed.

Cabalah: Path 3: Kether (God) to Tifereth (son)

Astrological Influence: The moon. The moon controls the tides and thus the emotions, imagination, moods, and rhythms. It reflects the light of the sun.

THE HIGH PRIESTESS IS THE MOON GODDESS. LIKE Isis, Ishtar, Artemis, and Astarte, she rules over the mysteries of women, the tides and currents, the emotions, and that which is hidden. Sophia, the goddess of wisdom, is also an aspect, as is the radiant light of Shekinah. Like the Christian Virgin Mary, she awaits her destiny. The Tarot's High Priestess sits between the sacred pillars: the black Pillar of Boaz (strength) and the white Pillar of Jachin (to establish). The pillars are the balance of darkness and light, positive and negative. She holds the secret knowledge of the Torah within her veils. She wears the jeweled, horned headdress of Isis. Her cool, serene, mysterious beauty reflects the qualities of silver, the metal associated with the moon. It beckons and attracts. What lies beyond the partially opened veil to the temple? One must learn the wisdom and knowledge to enter the temple and be initiated into the secrets she guards. She is receptive, in a sort of archetypal holding pattern. She can store an incident that happened years ago in her memory, and pull it out when everyone thought—and perhaps wished—it was long forgotten! Like Isis, she controls the tides and water. Her temperament is fluidic and governed by moods and deep thought. She is yin, the female aspect of the Godhead. She will shut off her light to you, then turn around and put a candle in the window. She is the virgin Eve who plucked the apple from the tree and handed it to Adam.

Classic Divinatory Meaning: Hidden meanings and mysteries. Duality. Education and knowledge. Higher learning. Female influence. Creative ability to be developed. Virginity.

Reversed: Vanity, immorality. Using feminine wiles in a destructive way.

Modern Meaning: A young or unmarried woman. A virgin. Feminine, artistic, creative ability. Beauty, knowledge, and learning. Sisterhood. Good taste. Mysterious attraction to a person, place, or things. Desire to solve a puzzling situation. Education, that which requires learning and training. Attraction to beauty. Desire. Active yin principle.

Reversed: A femme fatale. Dark secrets. Illicit affair. Strong attraction to the wrong person. Lack of interest in learning or aspiring higher. Misuse of femininity. Shallow, troubled person.

THE EMPRESS

Key 3

Numeral 3: Product, what has been created by union. Object of creation.

Hebrew Letter: Daleth: door. The door through which life enters the world.

Cabalah: Path 4: Hokmah (father) and Binah (mother).

Astrological Influence: Venus. Note the planet's symbol on her shield. Venus stands for love, creativity, harmony, and productivity.

THE EMPRESS IS THE GREAT GODDESS, THE EARTH Mother. The Golden Dawn referred to her as Isis, who as the "Giver of Corn," was also associated with the Greek Goddess Demeter. In the mysteries of Eleusis, she held the key to immortal life. The Empress is pregnant, surrounded by fertile, lush fields. Everything is in bloom and in fruition. In the background, a flowing waterfall unites the male and female, psyche and subconscious. Myrtle, the flower of Venus, adorns her cape along with fruits and plants. Her hair is golden, touched by the power of the sun rays. Like Venus, she is crowned with twelve stars. These stars represent the twelve signs of the zodiac, twelve months of the year and in Revelation, Chapter 12, "on

THE EMPRESS

her head a crown of twelve stars, she was with child" describes the Holy Mother. The Empress is the Pagan Goddess of Spring, The May Queen of plants, flowers, and fertility. According to Jung, the female archetype built over the years is creative, intuitive wisdom. She wears the calm expression of a fulfilled woman. She is depicted with the orbed scepter and wheat ready for harvest, symbol of the brevity of our life span.

Classic Divinatory Meaning: Creativity. Productivity. Fulfillment. Pregnancy. Great abundance. Bountiful crops and harvest. Success and luxury. Secure environment.

Reversed: Unproductive. Wasteful. Crops fail. Mental or physical illness. Poverty. Trouble with a pregnancy. Overgrown wilderness.

Modern Meaning: Motherhood, a mother, a grandmother. Very productive, creative, secure. Ability to create a warm and luxurious environment. Helpful and intuitive. Encouraging and productive. Fertility of mind and body. Blossoming, growing surroundings. Love. A matriarch. Pregnancy. Happy, warm, and loving person satisfied with life and willing to help others. Emotional, physical, spiritual fulfillment. Compassion.

Reversed: "Smother love." Overly anxious and therefore possessive. Trouble with a pregnancy. Interference. Infertility. Illness. Unproductive environment. Troubled home. Emotional manipulation. An enabler.

THE EMPEROR

THE EMPEROR

Key 4

Numeral 4: Logical reasoning, stability, and measurement.

Hebrew Letter: Heh: speech. Manifestation of thought communicated.

Cabalah: Path 5: Tifereth (son) crosses the abyss to Hokmah (father).

Astrological Influence: Aries. The ram governs reasoning and leadership.

Motto: "I exist/me first."

THE EMPEROR IS PATRIARCHAL AUTHORITY. HE IS logic and reason, the energetic force who organizes, governs, and directs. He is the father figure, the head of state, the one who controls the group. In his right hand is the Egyptian ankh, symbol of eternal life. It is also known as the Crux Ansata or Cross of Life. In his left hand rests the orb of the world he rules, governs, and dominates. The ram of Aries to his left enforces the aspects of organized structure. Since Aries is governed by fiery Mars, this warrior aspect is inherent in the Emperor. The flames in the background illustrate this fiery Mars energy and potential for destruction, war, and death. Like Osiris who was brought back to life by his wife Isis, the Emperor understands that in order to live he must control his own destructive instincts. He is, after all, logic personified. Jung refers to the archetypal father figure as the animus, opinionated and aggressive. The Emperor has evolved from hunter-gatherer to protector, creator of organized, civilized life, shaper of his world to ensure survival, order, and prosperity. Working together, the Empress and Emperor keep each other's archetypes in a system of checks and balances. The Emperor organizes the wild abundancy of the Empress's Mother Nature, and the Empress tempers the rigidity and warrior qualities of the Emperor.

Classic Divinatory Meaning: Leadership, government, kingship. Dominating type. Father. Patriarch. Logic. Systems. Intellectual. Mathematics. Maturity. Solid.

Reversed: Immature male. Poor leadership. Destruction.

Modern Meaning: Fatherhood, father, grandfather. A leader in business, industry, or government. A strict but solid, dependable person who runs a smooth ship. Great leadership abilities and an ability to spot people's talents and encourage or demand excellence. Mathematics, computers, logical systems. Well-run corporations. A born leader. One who creates order out of chaos. A collector of people, places, things. Intelligence.

Reversed: A control freak. Dominating male who is an aggressive "know it all." Refusal to listen, or listening when it is too late. Immature. Egotist. Insensitive. Rigid thinker. War maker. Closed mind leads to disaster.

THE HIEROPHANT

Key 5

Numeral 5: Need for order among chaos. Moral law in society. Spirit governing water, air, fire, earth.

Hebrew Letter: Vav: thought.

Cabalah: Path 6: Chokmah (wisdom) to Chesed (mercy).

Astrological Influence: Taurus. The bull is steadfast and secure. He is an earth sign that governs the physical world.

Motto: "I have/I indulge."

THE HIEROPHANT IS THE SPIRITUAL LEADER, master of religious ceremonies. In the Eleusinian mysteries he was called the "Revealer of Sacred Things." He gives the sign of benediction with his right hand. It is also the sign of esotericism. He holds the scepter of the triple cross which symbolizes ascent from the spiritual, physical, and emotional realms as well as the Trinity and God's influence on the planes above, below, and including the earthly, material plane. His triple crown repeats this theme. Crossing his chest are the keys to heaven and hell. The Hierophant is the spiritual guide, the moral leader, the keeper of external religion. His complete and flawless devotion to God and tradition is an example to society.

THE HIEROPHANT

Churches hold positions of political power and wealth, and there are many arguments they created to keep people in line, to prevent anarchy and chaos. Eliphas Levi wrote that the sign of esotericism that the Pope is giving casts a shadow with the head and horns of a devil, alluding to something sinister and dark. Religion can be used to oppress; the pilgrims left the comfort and security of home to travel across the Atlantic to start anew because of their oppression by the English church. Freud believed religion was designed to sublimate the sexual tendencies and to control people. Yet all societies seem to need to worship. Jung wrote that the instinct to worship is a compulsion imprinted on the psyche at birth. The benevolent gaze of Palladini's Hierophant portrays him as the spiritual counselor of the benefits of traditional religion and the path to righteousness, the bridge between God and man.

Classic Divinatory Meaning: Traditional religion, ceremonies, customs, rituals, and influence.

Reversed: Untraditional lifestyle. Free spirit, bohemian credo. Rejection of outworn religious customs. Nonconformist.

Modern Meaning: Involvement with the church or temple. Spiritual development. Traditional morality. Comfort from organized religion. A wedding, confirmation, baptism, or any ceremony that has to do with religion. Spiritual insight, a calling. Need to conform, to fit in. The traditional life.

Reversed: Disillusionment with religion. Rejecting pressure to conform. The desire to seek another way to worship, to develop spiritually. Untraditional person. Nonconformist. Rebellion.

THE LOVERS

THE LOVERS

Key 6

Numeral 6: Love, perfection, and harmony.

Hebrew Letter: Zayin: movement, sword. The sword cuts away old ties.

Cabalah: Path 7: Binah (mother) to Tifereth (son).

Astrological Influence: Gemini. The Gemini twins govern diversity, adaptability, duality, versatility, and choice.

Motto: "I think/I scheme."

THE BEAUTIFUL YOUNG LOVERS ARE UNITED IN A garden under the sun. They are soulmates, as harmonious as the Gemini twins. They have discovered themselves as individuals and made the choice of mate unique to their own personalities. They no longer need the emotional bonds and security of family. References to Adam and Eve, the forbidden fruit, the snake twining around the blossomed trees are displayed in sensual colors and in the fluidic, dreamlike scene. The plants seem to wrap around and encircle the two in nature's protection. The sun shines down upon them, bestowing heaven's blessings.

Some Tarot decks show the Lovers consulting with a Pope about marrying, others show a second woman indicating the man must chose between sacred and profane love. In any case, a choice has been made and perfect harmony between masculine and feminine has been accomplished. The love they share has created a third entity, a bond so strong and secure that there is no need or room for anybody else in this intimate world they have created. As with all choices, the Lovers will find new responsibilities. Eros has shot the arrow and nothing will be the same again.

Classic Divinatory Meaning: Choice. Attraction. Love. Trying to decide between two loves. Potentially good marriage partner.

Reversed: Parental interference in matters of the heart. Untrue lover. Wrong choice.

Modern Meaning: Lovers. Soulmates. A sincere and beautiful relationship. The choice between two or more lovers. Potential for marriage. Young at heart. Bliss. Honest and true communication and harmony. Two people in synchronicity. Emotional, intellectual, and physical attraction and love.

Reversed: Emotional distress over a love affair. Infidelity. Interference from family and friends. Jilted lover. Loneliness. Grief and trouble over a lost love. Separation

THE CHARIOT

Key 7

Numeral 7: Soul development, fate, destiny. Security. Luck.

Hebrew Letter: Cheth: sight.

Cabalah: Path 8: Binah (mother) to Geburah (strength).

Astrological Influence: Cancer. The crab is a receptive water sign with a tough exterior concealing and protecting his interior.

Motto: *"I feel/I brood."*

THE CHARIOT IS A CARD OF TRIUMPH, VICTORY, AND control of one's destiny. On the Cabalist Tree of Life, the Chariot victoriously crossed the abyss, which is not unlike a black hole in space for the soul. Palladini's charioteer resembles an Egyptian king, bold and upright. The courageous Charioteer wears the moon of his zodiac sign Cancer on his sleeve and he holds his sword upright and ready for defense. His Chariot's wheel burns with flames of gold, unstoppable and in motion. A bird sits on his shoulder with wings draped protectively around him. The bird embodies the spirit or ka of Horus, son of Isis and Osiris, who escaped triumphantly from all his

THE CHARIOT

perilous trials. The Charioteer will soon confront trouble, opposition, and tremendous obstacles. He is prepared, however, and has already proved himself capable.

This is the first of the Major Arcana to show a person in motion, traveling, forging his way. There is a super-awareness to Charioteer, which if unchecked can escalate into a tenseness. It is the struggle to maintain control of the self, the direction of one's vehicle, the base instincts and desires that tug at the soul and try to pull the Charioteer off track.

Classic Divinatory Meaning: Conquest, victory, success. Travel. Great achievements. Control of one's interests.

Reversed: Stumbling along without direction, loss of vision. Lack of control.

Modern Meaning: Success. Protecting one's interests. A person in control of the direction their life is taking. Smart decisions. Tough negotiations successfully worked out. Adequate preparation. Travel that will be of great importance. Excellent preparation combined with luck ensures a successful outcome. Actual vehicles, planes, ships.

Reversed: To fall off the path. Lack of success. Inadequate preparation. Loss of direction. Weakness. Vulnerability. Possibility of travel accidents. Need to protect oneself. Business or job losses for adults; prematurely leaving school or getting involved with bad influences for young people. A need to get back on track and protect oneself, quickly.

STRENGTH

STRENGTH

Key 8

Numeral 8: Strength, health, rhythm, balance, intensity.

Hebrew Letter: Teth: hearing.

Cabalah: Path 9: Geburah (strength) to Chesed (mercy).

Astrological Influence: Leo. The message of the lion is strength, self-righteousness, and dominance over negativity.

Motto: "I will/I pretend."

A GENTLE WOMAN EXERTS QUIET STRENGTH TO subdue the lion, King of Beasts. The lion symbolizes the unruly, dark, and primitive side of our souls. The cultured woman shows this energy can be tamed and channeled into something useful. The passionate instinctive stirrings in man would create havoc and ruin if left to run wild. The refinement cultivated in civilization shown is personified in the woman from India who tames the savage beast with little effort. She has even managed to place a garland of flowers around his neck to symbolize the union of their combined desires. A.E. Waite, a member of the Golden Dawn, described the sexual nature of the card by pointing out fortitude is connected with the Divine Mystery of

Union. The lemniscate above her head is the one that appeared over the Magician's head. It is the symbol of the harmonious universe, all forces working together infinitely, eternal life. The female is helping tame the wild animal forces in the psyche. The lion will not weaken from her influence. The primitive nature can't be ignored. It has to be acknowledged and effectively sublimated to allow for cultivation and refinement.

Classic Divinatory Meaning: Strength, good health, fortitude. Inner resources. Persistence and fortitude.

Reversed: Weakness, ill health.

Modern Meaning: Strength of body and mind. Good health. Careful attention to health and fitness. Courage. Fortitude. Healthy body, healthy mind. Ability to control the volatile, instinctive urges and channel them into good use. Dynamic energy. Gentle but firm rulership.

Reversed: Weakness, mental and physical. Need for rejuvenation. Giving in to destructive needs and not having the willpower of strength or mind to stop. Bad dreams.

THE HERMIT

Key 9

Numeral 9: Mystical number. Completion of a cycle and attainment after a struggle.

Hebrew Letter: Yod: work.

Cabalah: Path 10: Chesed (mercy) to Tiphereth (beauty).

Astrological Influence: Virgo. The Virgin stands for perfection, purification, and the realization of goals.

Motto: "I study/I worry."

THE HERMIT HAS RETREATED FROM SOCIETY. HE IS cloaked in esoteric secrecy, yet he holds forth the Light of Perfect Knowledge to illuminate others. He is willing to share his wisdom, but the seeker must go to him. His cloak is purple, the Christian color of the martyr in total submission to God. He has rejected the trappings of the material plane. He has only his cloak for protection, a lantern to light the way and his walking stick for comfort. His long white beard makes him the archetypal "old wise man" who holds the knowledge only time and experience can deliver. He is the person who continues the solitary search for truth. Research by Jung concludes that when one is alone for an extended period of time, the psyche

THE HERMIT

produces visions and revelations. This is what the Apostle John experienced when he had the series of enlightening dreams and visions described in Revelation 4:7. It is the place in the mind where the artist goes to meditate before putting the brush to canvas. The archetype of the wise old man reflects profound thought and clear, bright intellect. His knowledge is incomprehensible to most, so he is content to share the physical plane with man, but he is always a step apart.

Classic Divinatory Meaning: Attainment of wisdom. Inner knowledge. Spiritual illumination. Advice and counsel from a wise soul. Ability to counsel. The need to step back from society and soul-search. Withdrawl.

Reversed: Refusal to listen to one's own inner voice or the wise counsel from others. Mental breakdown. Comprehension difficulties. Closed mind.

Modern Meaning: Spiritual awareness and development. The need to retreat from society to soul-search and find a deeper meaning to life. Seeking counsel for the purpose of reflection. Self-sufficient person. Self-imposed exile. Lonely but content. Intellectual person. Completing a cycle and moving on to something higher. Mental or physical retreat.

Reversed: Not retreating for much-needed soul-searching causes problems and neuroses. There is a need for time alone—take it. Avoiding thinking through important issues. Inability to solve problems, writer's block, a dry period for the creative person. Depression. Failure to see the light.

THE WHEEL OF FORTUNE

THE WHEEL OF FORTUNE

Key 10

Numeral 10: Individual personality with limitless energy.

Hebrew Letter: Kaph: grace.

Cabalah: Path 11: Chesed (mercy) to Netzach (victory).

Astrological Influence: Jupiter. Jupiter governs circular motion, reason, and comprehension. It symbolizes the prophet, expansion, and freedom.

THE WHEEL REVOLVES AROUND THE FOUR elements shown clockwise as fire, air, water, and earth. The letters T, A, R, O are spelled in capital letters around the wheel with the Hebrew letters of the Tetragrammaton in between. Together they spell out the name of God, reminding that whatever happens, good or bad, is all in the Divine Plan. Clockwise within the wheel are the four elements that make up life on the earthly plane: air, water, earth, fire. The Wheel of Fortune shows the cyclical nature of life on earth; the universal principles of growth, completion, decline, renewal. The karmic nature of what has been done or started has come full circle to completion. Loose ends are never really loose. They must be woven into the wheel as it spins. All beginnings must have endings, the seasons come and go, as do our periods of triumphs and failures. The cyclical rhythm of life does not allow for one to be on top of the wheel with everything going wonderfully forever. In that same regard, the bad times will inevitably pass, too. The wheel is ever-spinning. The free will to pick and choose exists only in the mysterious circle of our fate and destiny. We have to adapt to the ever-changing environment of nature and the collective consciousness of humankind. Like the snakes pictured, we have to shed the skins we have outgrown and keep moving. What happens in the future depends on the sum of past events. As ye hath sown, so shall ye reap.

Classic Divinatory Meaning: Good fortune and luck. Success. Fate and destiny. Laws of nature and probability. Karmic law. Change for the better.

Reversed: Bad luck or fortune. Downward motion. Paying for mistakes. Troubles. Change for the worse.

Modern Divinatory Meaning: Good fortune. Success. A cycle of gain and happiness. Everything works out. Efforts of the past come to fruition. Good work and deeds of the past are rewarded now. Karma, fate, and destiny. Peak time of happiness and glory.

Reversed: Bad luck, hopes crashed, dreams trampled. Bad deeds or unstable efforts in the past have come up to haunt you now. Paying dues or plain old bad luck.

JUSTICE

Key 11

Numeral 11: Positive action by the individual. Mystical awareness. Balance between good and evil.

Hebrew Letter: Lamed: coition.

Cabalah: Path 12: Geburah (strength) to Tiphereth (son).

Astrological Influence: Libra. The scales of balance are the symbol of Libra along with the attributes of justice, order, balance, and harmony.

Motto: "I cooperate/I procrastinate."

JUSTICE, PERSONIFIED AS A VEILED WOMAN, contemplates a leaf and coins on the scales of balance. Like the High Priestess, she sits between two pillars, but this time the golden sword of justice appears from the veiled heavens. The double-edged sword cuts through fact and fantasy to determine the truth. Responsibility for one's actions and their outcome will be determined. The scales of balance intimate justice is not black and white; it is relative and unique to the situation and individual personalities involved. The pillars in the background represent the polarization of opposites and the static tension between them which needs to be equalized. The

JUSTICE

qualities of equilibrium, balance, and harmony don't always occur naturally and that is where the female figure as mediator is needed. She wears the green robe of Venus's love and understanding over a red robe, the color of the war and turmoil of Mars. She weighs the warring sides with compassion and the wisdom of a higher plane as indicated by the double-edged sword. Key 11 reminds us we are responsible for our actions which will be weighed and balanced not only on the physical plane, but on a higher plane as well.

Classic Divinatory Meaning: Justice. A fair end to a lawsuit. Law. Good judgement. Foresight and keen awareness. Equality.

Reversed: Injustice. Legal losses. Legal complications.

Modern Meaning: Justice and a fair outcome of lawsuits and legal matters. All matters pertaining to law. A fair and observant person with the ability to judge. Foresight. A chance to set matters straight. Courts and law offices. Deliberation. Mediation.

Reversed: Misuse of law. Injustice. Legal complications. Losses. Excessive penalty.

THE HANGED MAN

THE HANGED MAN

Key 12

Numeral 12: Beginning of reasoning and completion.

Hebrew Letter: Mem: primordial waters.

Cabalah: Path 13: Geburah (strength) to Hod (splendor).

Astrological Influence: Neptune. Neptune rules the sea, the imagination, and intuition. He is associated with the mystics and has both spiritual and escapist trends.

THE HANGED MAN, SUSPENDED UPSIDE DOWN FROM a tree, stares ahead as though in a trance. His crossed leg forms the sign of the cross. Three triangles, symbolic of the Trinity, are formed by his legs and arms. The nimbus or glow of spiritual illumination and surrender to the Holy Spirit emanates around his head. This man has come to a complete stop and surrender. The relaxed, peaceful expression on his face indicates the surrender was anticipated. He hangs on a T cross ripe with fruit and flowers. In medieval prints, Christ was often depicted hanging from a flowering tree. This connection reveals something holy, a sacrifice to God, a surrender leading to the resurrection. The Hanged Man has also been connected to the northern European Odin, god of magic, inspiration, war, poetry, and death. Odin, to win mastery

over the magic rune stones, hung on a windy tree for nine
nights as a sacrifice to himself. This act indicates submission to and acceptance of knowledge. A literal reversal
of the path one was on must take place before ascending
to something higher. The triangle shape also indicates an
instinctual rise to the top; the ascension of all things.
Shown inverted on the Hanged Man, it shows a descension
into matter and then rising again, or more literally, a
descent into hell and back up again.

Classic Divinatory Meaning: Sacrifice for a noble cause.
Wisdom, self-sacrifice, surrender to a Higher Force.
Reversal. Suspended decisions.

Reversed: Stagnation. A personality stuck in a material,
physical world unable to grasp any higher meaning of or
in life. Self-absorption.

Modern Meaning: Sacrifice. Suspended decisions. Waiting
period. Feeling like one is in limbo, although there
really is a change occurring within oneself. Confession,
surrender to a higher force. Nothing can be forced to
happen at this time. A surrender to the inner, higher self
has to be allowed to happen before nature and destiny can
proceed along its course. A new direction. A complete
reversal of things.

Reversed: Stagnation, lethargy. Nothing works out right.
Following a barren or fruitless pattern that no longer fits
or works.

DEATH

Key 13

Numeral 13: A number considered unlucky because it is haunted by fear and superstition.

Hebrew Letter: Nun: smell.

Cabalah: Path 14: Tiphereth (son) to Netzach (victory).

Astrological Influence: Scorpio. The scorpion rules the reproductive organs, birth, and death.

Motto: "I desire/I suspect."

A GHOSTLY SKELETON RIDES IN ON A WHITE HORSE partially devoured by snakes slithering up from the dark night. Volcanoes erupt and smoke fills the violent red skies. Yet, amidst this bleak landscape, a torn black flag bearing the Mystic Rose, a symbol of life, offers hope. Death's glowing eye defiantly stares out at the viewer, demanding an acknowledgment of this fate that awaits us all. Everything born of this world reaches its peak then starts the degeneration process. "For dust thou art, and unto dust shalt thou return." (Genesis 3:16) The white rose indicates hope for a new life ahead. When the body can no longer function as the vessel for the soul, death occurs for the physical form but the soul moves on to a

DEATH

new home. Plants and animals all return to the earth and new life springs forth in a cycle of degeneration and regeneration. Death in the Tarot stands for this transformation and renewal. It is a card that can initially bring chills, but like its number 13, it is necessary for nature's orderly progression. The alchemists referred to the process of life after death as putrefaction. When their mixtures were at the point of rot and stench (note the Hebrew letter associated to Death stands for "smell"), they would regenerate new life.

Classic Divinatory Meaning: Death, rebirth, renewal. Psychic rebirth. Termination.

Reversed: Slow change. Things aren't working out.

Modern Meaning: Transformation for the better. Renewal, rebirth. A situation that has been difficult to endure is ending. The way will soon be clear to begin anew. Fresh starts, new insight, and hope. A loss that brings sadness, then understanding. There may be a death but other cards in the reading will clarify whether it is of a person, place, or thing. An old friendship or project is renewed.

Reversed: Bad habits and/or reckless behavior that can lead to death. Stagnation. Insurmountable situation. Putting off ending something that has outworn its time. Trapped or stuck physically or mentally. Need to reboot and inject some life into your existence.

TEMPERANCE

TEMPERANCE

Key 14

Numeral 14: Beginning of logical reason for the organized, spiritual person.

Hebrew Letter: Samekh: sleep.

Cabalah: Path 15: Tiphereth (son) to Yesod (foundation).

Astrological Influence: Sagittarius. The archer has a restless intellect and rules the hips and thighs, which support the upper weight of the body.

Motto: "*I understand/I exaggerate.*"

AN ARCHANGEL POURS THE WATERS OF LIFE between two gold cups. This act of flowing is symbolic of equalizing the stream of thought between the conscious and subconscious. Temperance is the exact mix, the harmonizing of the psychic and material, a synthesis of all things.

The flowing of water can also mean the communication from mind to mind. Angels are messengers of God who are the links between heaven and earth. They are believed to help us in times of trouble or danger, communicating telepathically. Paul Foster Case wrote that water was the "mind stuff" and the cosmos was made up of vibrations which could be tempered. Edison, when asked how he invented the light bulb, was reported to reply that thoughts are out there, he just happened to tap into them. The channeling of information into the mind of humankind could be "the calling" people hear to enter the priesthood or other vocations. It occurs as an inner voice that seems to guide us to make good decisions or to warn us of impending trouble. Balance, moderation, control, and patience clear the static between the subconscious and the conscious mind.

Classic Divinatory Meaning: Temperance, balance, control, and modification. Diplomacy. An even-tempered person.

Reversed: Tendency to overdo things. Poor combinations. Competing desires and interests. Extremist.

Modern Meaning: Effective management skills. Well-balanced person. Temperance. Diplomacy. An even-tempered person. Perfect harmony for the artist, musician. Creative inventions for people in the sciences. Excellent communication skills. Insightful, intuitive. Psychic ability. Peacemaker. A person in the healing professions. The act of healing. Cooperation. Partnerships. Smooth-running ventures. The ability to successfully adapt to changing situations.

Reversed: Mismanagement. Poor combinations. Overindulgence. Addictions. Poor health. Unbalanced personality. Trouble with communications, relationships. Misdiagnosis of a medical problem. A person "out of tune" or "out of synch" with him or herself, who unintentionally bungles the life of another. Extremist.

THE DEVIL

Key 15

Numeral 15: Individual suffering in a whirlwind of chaos and confusion.

Hebrew Letter: Ayin: eye, anger.

Cabalah: Path 16: Tiphereth (son) to Hod (splendor).

Astrological Influence: Capricorn. The goat is the practical materialist who governs the knees.

Motto: "I use/I inhibit."

THE GOAT-HEADED DEVIL AWAITS WITH HIS CHAIN to capture the weak. He is an aggressive demon that does not wait passively for his victims. He pursues them with a vengeance, offering temptations tailor-made to appeal to the particular soul he seeks. He is the antithesis of the Magician who uses his power for good. He is depicted as half-man to show that the weaknesses he seeks to tap into already exist in man. This also illustrates his infamous ability to adapt his appearance as a disguise.

Hatred, anger, violence, ignorance, cruelty, lust—all these unbridled emotions can send one whirling in a downward spiral of chaos and confusion. The Devil is related to the Greek goat Pan who lured people to wild

THE DEVIL

nature and untamed sexuality with the promise of eternal pleasure of the senses. The Devil's astrological sign is Capricorn, who is ruled by Saturn, and whose negative attributes are that which cause things to go in reverse. His other names include Satan and Lucifer, the fallen angel whose name means "light bearer." The Tarot's Devil reminds us that obsessive potential does exist in man, but the energy can be controlled and directed into something positive. The greenish scales on his body link him to Set, the Egyptian god of Evil, who appeared as an alligator or a snake. His clawed hands are like those of Tiamat, the Babylonian goddess of chaos. Banished Lucifer no longer wears angel wings. They are now batlike, symbolic of the rodent's night flights and visits to the sleeping or unaware mind.

Classic Divinatory Meaning: Disorder, chaos, and ruin. Enslavement to a negative person, place, or thing. Violence. Revolution. Black magic. Regression.

Reversed: Release from bondage. Healing.

Modern Meaning: Drug addiction. Alcoholism. Sexual perversion. Unbridled anger, violence, lust. Dominance. Evil. That which rots. Cancer, disease. Sorrow, depression. Chaos, confusion. Obsessions. Lost soul. Selfish, materialistic tendencies. Psychosis. Entangled in a web of evil.

Reversed: Freedom. Healing. Extrication from a negative force. Triumph over an obsession or an addiction. Return to health and equilibrium. This card can appear when someone has just escaped a near-ruinous, even fatal situation. Release or escape from a horrible place or relationship.

THE TOWER

THE TOWER

Key 16

Numeral 16: Beginning of perfection. The way to harmony.

Hebrew Letter: Pe: mouth.

Cabalah: Path 17: Hod (splendor) to Netzach (mercy).

Astrological Influence: Mars. This planet has both destructive and constructive tendencies; one makes way for the other.

A TOWER HIGH ON A HILL HAS BEEN STRUCK BY lightning and flames spill out from within. The lightning hits in a split second, a momentary insight or realization that everything thought to be true is false. The current path is suddenly a prison, a tower built upon false hopes and incorrect assumptions; and now the truth strikes and nothing will be the same again. The loftiness of the tower points to human pride and arrogance, and the cracks lead to the inevitable fall. The phallic symbol of the tower foretells new creation, but this time with insight. Lightning used to be considered the touch of God's hand coming down from the heavens to illuminate and enlighten. The black night and steep cliffs enhance the bleakness and desperation of this card. On the Cabalist

Tree of Life, the Tower's path is between Devil and Death. A total breaking down, a meltdown of sorts, has to occur to make way for the transformation and reorganization. The change is traumatic but necessary. The green branches on the trees point to new growth, a new phase of life.

Classic Divinatory Meaning: Disasters, catastrophes, wars, accidents. Divorce. Bankruptcy. Disaster in the home or business. Sudden realization or inspiration that upsets old ideas. A sudden catastrophe that changes everything.

Reversed: The same, but with less intensity. Lack of insight. Imprisonment. Enforced visits.

Modern Meaning: Divorce. Bankruptcy. Floods, natural disasters. War. Disruptions of an extreme nature. Trouble in the home or workplace that leads to dissolution. The sudden ending of a way of life, business, or relationship. Realization that things can no longer continue the way they are. Traumatic but inevitable change. Emotional upheaval.

Reversed: The same, but with less intensity. Warnings. Problems left unsolved will escalate to gigantic proportions. Staying in an undesirable situation. Enduring difficulties.

THE STAR

Key 17

Numeral 17: Beginning of positive action triggered by a philosophical, spiritual outlook. Magical luck.

Hebrew Letter: Tzaddi: fish hook.

Cabalah: Path 18: Netzach (mercy) to Yesod (foundation).

Astrological Influence: Aquarius: The water carrier is an intuitive activist, analytical, and interested in groups.

Motto: "I know/I'm unreliable."

A NAKED FEMALE SUBMERGED IN WATER POURS liquid from two cups. She resembles Ishtar, the Babylonian goddess of fertility and love whose name interprets as "star." The water she pours is the *amrita,* the dew of immortality in the Hindu religion. She is also Aquarius, pouring the waters of inspiration, peace, and benevolence. A bird in a tree watches over her, symbolic of the soul's ability to rise above. The tree, rooted in soil, brings the inspiration to our earthly plane.

This is the card of illumination and hope, of spiritual love and guidance. A Star shone over the manger to guide the Wise Men to the Savior. Astronomers use stars to map out the heavens. Astrologers seek answers from the stars

THE STAR

to help guide life on earth. The Star is our guide; it shines through the darkness of night. Water historically symbolizes the continuity of life, the subconscious mind, revival, and baptism. The Hebrew letter Tzaddi stands for "fish hook," which would imply dropping the line into the waters of the subconscious to search and discover. Nakedness implies truth, purity, and the revelation of nature's mysteries.

Classic Divinatory Meaning: Insight. Hope. Open mind. High intelligence. Unselfish aid and help.

Reversed: Narrow mind. Lack of insight. Pessimist. Dullness of mind.

Modern Meaning: Insight. Hope. Highly intelligent person. Places of learning. New solutions to old problems. Quick thinking. Problem-solving ability. A spiritual guide. People are willing to help. Ability to turn wishes into realities for self and others.

Reversed: Lack of insight. Slow to learn. Bogged down by the trivial. Dullness of mind. Attention given to unimportant areas. Slow to seek or extend help to or from others.

THE MOON

THE MOON

Key 18

Numeral 18: The individual, steeped in intense emotion, has difficulties sorting things through.

Hebrew Letter: Qoph: head.

Cabalah: Path 19: Netzach (victory) to Malkuth (kingdom).

Astrological Influence: Pisces. The fish are psychic, reflective, mysterious, and reflect qualities of all twelve zodiac signs.

Motto: "I believe/I escape."

THE SILVERY CRESCENT MOON GLOWS IN THE black night, the top of its circular form outlined by the shadowy rays of reflected light. Drops of light ("Yods" in Hebrew) rain over the countryside, signifying the descent of the life force into the material plane. The Moon's path on the Tree of Life takes it down through the psychic realm into the earthly plane. The Golden Dawn wrote that this card is connected to the soul entering the earthly body. It is now hidden and secrets abound. The two towers mark the gateway to the unknown. A crayfish crawls up from the murky waters signifying evolution, the properties of Cancer and of depths unknown. The Moon's faint light reflects thoughts from the subconscious and the imagination. It barely lights the path which summons primitive fears dredged up from instinct and vague memories from the past. The Moon controls the tides and our deep emotions. It causes dogs to howl, influences women's reproductive systems, draws out creativity—and also madness. Instinctively, we are drawn to follow the path of the Moon, to stare at it in the night sky, to let it hypnotize and draw out our untamed imagination.

Classic Divinatory Meaning: Solitude. Imagination and creativity. Hidden talents emerge. Psychic ability. Intuitive reasoning. Mystery. Danger. Hidden enemies. Secret loves.

Reversed: Imagination grounded by reality. Mishaps. Unforeseen perils. Secrets revealed.

Modern Meaning: Psychic ability. Intuition. Mystery. Love of mystery, secrets. Creative person, emotional, and prone to moodiness. Artistic talents. Compulsive urge to create. Hidden talents emerge. Escapist. The compulsion to escape into roles, the theater, arts, music, journeys, expeditions. Intuitive reasoning. Dreams. Messages. Enemies. Clandestine affairs.

Reversed: Mishaps, perils. Nightmares. Intense worries. Inexplicable sadness or irritability. Angst. Frustration. Mysteries solved. Deceit exposed.

THE SUN

Key 19

Numeral 19: The individual attains the goal. Sacred significance. Courage, brotherly love.

Hebrew Letter: Resh: fertility.

Cabalah: Path 20: Hod (splendor) to Yesod (foundation).

Astrological Influence: Sun. The sun symbolizes power, energy, dignity, health, personality, leadership, and God's love.

A BRIGHT, BOLD SUN WITH A FACE IN THE IMAGE OF man shines forth its rays. Drops of Yod (the life force) radiate into shimmering waters of rebirth and continuity. A lotus flower in full bloom signifies the microcosm within the macrocosm. The Sun's light offers warmth and security, a cheerfulness after having navigated the way along the shadowy path of the moon. Nothing is dim or concealed here; we can clearly see the way to our Highest Goal. This is the key of clear sight, the full light of day, the unrestrained joy and happiness one feels in childhood. It is a card of innocence and rejoicing.

The Sun is the source of power and light. The Egyptians and Native Americans referred to it as their Supreme Being. The Sun is the power in the manifest world and

THE SUN

lights the way to the world beyond. Divine Light, which unites all intelligence and knowledge gained on the earthly journey. The human spirit is liberated and the regenerated personality unites with the Whole.

Classic Divinatory Meaning: Achievements. Goals met. Success assured. Happy families. Good marriage. Joy. Contentment. Completion of studies, projects. Happiness. Enjoyment of the little things in life.

Reversed: Unhappiness. Broken marriages, broken contracts. Projects gone sour. Feigned happiness. Elusive happiness.

Modern Meaning: Achievements. Goals met. Graduations. Weddings. Happy marriage. Successful completion. Great joy. Celebrations. Clear conscience. Enjoyable time of life. Liberation. Winnings. Effervescence. Zest of life attracts friends and opportunities.

Reversed: Dutifully fulling obligations without enjoyment. Plans goes sour. Lost loves, agreements, contracts. Simulated enjoyment.

THE LAST JUDGEMENT

THE LAST JUDGEMENT

Key 20

Numeral 20: Adding on or to another force in a higher plane.

Hebrew Letter: Shin: primordial fire.

Cabalah: Path 21: Hod (splendor) to Malkuth (kingdom).

Astrological Influence: Pluto. The dark lord; the purgatory or dwelling place of departed souls.

AN ANGEL BLOWS THE TRUMPET THAT AWAKENS the souls of the dead. In the Middle Ages, it was known as the Day of Wrath, when Christ would appear in the sky and send the departed to heaven or hell. St. Paul in 1 Corinthians wrote, "...we shall all be changed, in a moment, in the twinkling of an eye, at the last trumpet. For the trumpet will sound, and the dead will be raised imperishable, and we shall be changed." The trumpet awakens the soul for resurrection. The banner has the cross of equal sides, a reconciliation of opposites and unity of man and woman; God and earth.

This is a card of judgements, reunions, new life, a future based on the past although completely free from it. The Hebrew letter associated with Judgement, Shin, stands for fire: great light, warmth, and passion, but also destruction to ashes. Shin also refers to the Holy Spirit. The alchemists referred to the process of reducing something by fire to ash as calcination. After death the physical body can be reduced to ashes by cremation. The symbolic result here is the soul's liberation. Physical death does not have to occur. As the Archangel Michael said, "We can rise from the grave of our old dead self now, while still in the physical body, if our ears are not deaf to the trumpet call from on high."

Classic Divinatory Meaning: Judgement. Reawakening. A time to make amends. Serenity. Making peace with yourself, family, and friends. Fulfillment. Healing.

Reversed: Failures on a spiritual, emotional level. Weakness of body and mind. Ill health. Fear of death and what lies beyond.

Modern Meaning: A time to atone for actions. Judgement is imminent. You are being judged and also judging others. "Seeing the light." Awakening. Serenity. A time to make peace. Healing. Fulfillment. Setting affairs in order.

Reversed: Fear of death. Fear of being accountable for actions. Avoidance of responsibilities. Guilt. Ill health. Unhappiness in old age. Severe depression. Not making the most out of life and not enjoying life.

THE WORLD

Key 21

Numeral 21: Completion, unification, blending with the whole.

Hebrew Letter: Tav: peace.

Cabalah: Path 22: Yesod (foundation) to Malkuth (kingdom).

Astrological Influence: Saturn. Time and the absorption of all expressions into itself, truth, and learning are Saturn's attributes.

A LIGHT, ETHEREAL WOMAN DANCES INSIDE A flowering wreath. The veil that flows over her naked body is translucent, no longer the opaque veils that guarded her secrets in previous Tarot cards. Here all is revealed, there is a peacefulness in the dancer's expression and her whole being seems to glimmer. The flowering wreath recalls the unity between god and nature and a victorious ending. The dancer can be Mother Nature herself, Eve who danced in the Garden of Eden, or Shekinah, the feminine aspect of God. The magical wands she holds balance positive and negative. If the Major Arcana are read as a book of life from beginning to end, this card would be the just rewards of Heaven. On the earthly plane, it would be complete

THE WORLD

peace and harmony within ourselves and the world we have created around us. There is a protective nature to this card implied by the security and infinity of the circular wreath around the woman. Four as a number of security is reflected in the amount of birds who sit at each corner. Paul Foster Case refers to this card as the "cosmic consciousness," the state of being one with nature, achieving immortality. The World is the synthesis of all things, the completion of work, the spiritual evolution, and the return home.

Classic Divinatory Meaning: Triumph. Eternal life. Peace and joy in a new home. Rewards. Cosmic consciousness. Assured success. Travel. Joyous return home. Completion.

Reversed: Failures. Plans dashed. Hard work for naught. Unrewarded efforts.

Modern Meaning: Triumphs. Rewards. Victories. "On top of the world" in your career or home. Assured success. Reaching the ultimate goal. Completion. Joyous return home. Travel. Cosmic consciousness. Peace and joy in a new home. The dream house. The ideal place to be. A place to do perfect work. True self-expression.

Reversed: Earthbound soul. Stagnation. Plans ruined. Trouble in the home. Strong attachment to a place or object. Refusal to leave a situation or place that no longer exists as you once knew it.

THE MINOR ARCANA

THE SUIT OF SWORDS

ACE OF SWORDS

ACE OF SWORDS

A GLOVED HAND EMERGES FROM A CLOUD, holding forth an ornate gold sword topped by a crown. Thistles twine around the double-edged sword of higher justice. The crown denotes rulership, authority, the kingdom. White clouds are silhouetted against a black sky. Stars twinkle and a crescent moon shines. This striking imagery conveys the power, aggression, and boldness of the suit.

Meaning: Aggression. Birth of a strong-willed child. Masculine. Authority, aggression in the pursuit of excellence. Courage and fortitude. The beginning of a noble cause. Belief in ideas. Triumph. Championship. Force. Hard intelligence. Artificial intelligence (computers, scientific equipment, calculators). Analysis.

Reversed: Weakness of will. Negative force. Impotence. Tyranny. Disaster. Force used to destroy.

TWO OF SWORDS

TWO OF SWORDS

A FEMALE FIGURE DRESSED IN A PROTECTIVE SUIT of mail holds two crossed swords. The blindfold suggests she cannot see; however, her free hands imply she can remove the blindfold. Trees stand fast on green hills in background. Dusk falls, lending a purple haze to the partially cloudy sky. A crescent moon in the center emphasizes the symmetry of the clouds, trees, swords, and hands.

Meaning: A difficult decision must be made. Pros and cons seem to have equal strength. The crossed swords indicate a truce, but the blindfold warns it may be temporary or not what it appears to be. Stalemate. Balance but not without tension. Deadlock.

Reversed: A wrong move and a decision you must live with. Make new friends and create new circumstances. Disastrous results from an impetuous decision.

THREE OF SWORDS

THREE OF SWORDS

A HEART PIERCED BY THREE SWORDS HANGS suspended in a cloudy, rainy sky. The crescent moon in the center relates it to the decision forced in the Two of Swords. The wounded heart denotes intense sorrow and the raindrops fall like tears.

Meaning: Heartache and sorrow. Tears and anguish. Forced separations, loss of love or loved ones. Loneliness. Emotional upheaval. Difficult, trying time. Intense emotional pain or scars. Betrayals. Disappointment in love.

Reversed: Sorrow to a lesser degree. Confusion. Possible danger of position being compromised. Disorder. Broken promises. Disruptions. Quarreling, conflict, war.

FOUR OF SWORDS

FOUR OF SWORDS

A KNIGHT HAS TAKEN OFF HIS HELMET AND NOW sleeps on a coffin-like slab. The ornate decoration and Egyptian columns indicate he is in a sanctuary rather than a tomb. Three swords are suspended in the night sky outside the window. One sword rests upon him.

Meaning: Convalescence. Recuperation after illness or war. Hospitalization. A retreat to rejuvenate. Recovery. Healings. In some cases, seclusion.

Reversed: Return to the outside world. Back into action although in a different capacity. New relationships.

FIVE OF SWORDS

FIVE OF SWORDS

A COMPETENT-LOOKING KNIGHT, STILL DRESSED from battle, gathers up swords strewn across a field. At first glance, it appears he has survived a battle that has taken place. However, the night sky could indicate he has waited until dark to sneak into enemy territory and steal their weapons. The fact that he is alone could mean he does not have the support of his regiment.

Meaning: A sneak. The upper hand was achieved by unfair means. Cheating. A troublemaker working in the shadows. Behind-the-scenes trickery. Craftiness and unfair gain. Illegal actions. Someone working diligently to undermine and sabotage. A warning to beware of harm from a person of this nature.

Reversed: Dishonor. Cowardice. Branded. Loss of reputation. Losses, defeats, humiliations. Mourning. Picking up the pieces literally and/or figuratively after a disaster.

SIX OF SWORDS

SIX OF SWORDS

TWO HOODED AND CAPED FIGURES TRAVEL BY night in a hand-crafted boat. They are leaving rippled waters which indicate a troubled time and row into smooth waters and promising green mountains. The clouds seem to clear up closer to their destination. There is a quiet solemnity to this journey portrayed by the hunched and heavily wrapped figures.

Meaning: Travel to a safer, calmer place. Smooth progress away from difficulties. Leaving a troubled situation. The straightening out of affairs. Smooth sailing ahead. Solving problems and moving on to better circumstances. This can also mean a move, or a long journey by boat. Moving to more pleasant surroundings. Help from a caring friend.

Reversed: Stuck in an intolerable situation. No immediate way out of unfortunate circumstances at this point. Unpleasant surprises. Uncomfortable situations at home, at work, or both.

SEVEN OF SWORDS

SEVEN OF SWORDS

A MAN SEEMS TO BE HURRYING ACROSS A FIELD at night holding five swords. He has left two behind, perhaps because he couldn't carry them all. He is not dressed for war and he looks out at the viewer implying he is aware he could be seen. Since he is in a field at night, it would seem he doesn't want to be caught taking the swords.

Meaning: Theft. The thief has spied the goods, made the plan, and now acts out the robbery. Untrustworthy people around the home. Unstable, potentially dangerous person. Injuries. Victimization. Crime. A warning to guard against this.

Reversed: Partial recovery of stolen goods. Thief caught. Surrender. Confession of crime.

EIGHT OF SWORDS

EIGHT OF SWORDS

BOUND AND BLINDFOLDED, A WOMAN STANDS captive between eight swords. Storm clouds gather in a night sky. The surreal color and texture of the ground suggest the woman could be a victim of her own imagination. Tormented by thoughts, she is unable to free herself. Whether real or imagined, the image is one of captivity and imprisonment.

Meaning: Imprisoned and immobilized. Held captive without any immediate way out. Feeling lost and outside with no clue how to get back home. This card can be a state of mind, an emotional and intellectual paralysis of sorts, or it could indicate someone is in prison or a prison-like place. Lack of freedom or hope. Uncertainty. Unable to extricate oneself from negative entanglements. Hospitalization.

Reversed: Release from prison. Relaxation. Relief. New movement toward a productive life.

NINE OF SWORDS

NINE OF SWORDS

A TROUBLED WOMAN HOLDS HER HEAD IN HER hands as she sits up in bed. She cannot sleep with nine swords of trouble and strife looming above her. The sharp, jagged patterns around her bed evoke a nervous tension inconducive to peaceful sleep.

Meaning: A worried mind. Insomnia. Nightmares. Worries that escalate in intensity at night. Angst. Misery and suffering. Intense worry. Possible loss of a loved one. Loneliness and desolation. Dread.

Reversed: Fear, suspicion, and loneliness stemming from unfortunate, bad experiences in the past. Unable to completely recover. Take one day at a time. Remember, this too shall pass.

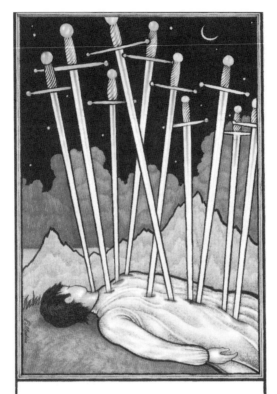

TEN OF SWORDS

TEN OF SWORDS

OVERTAKEN BY TEN SWORDS, THE VICTIM LAYS
stabbed and bleeding on a high hill. Ice-topped mountains
and dark clouds swirl in the background. The sword's
negative side of violence and destruction is epitomized by
a youth stopped in the prime of life. Blood symbolizes the
final result of a time of extreme pain and suffering.

Meaning: Sudden endings. Misfortune, trouble, anger,
strife culminating in a disaster. This could be the ending
of a troubled time or an actual death. Carefully note other
cards around it to prevent unnecessary worry. It could be
someone has lost a loved one to an unexpected, untimely
death such as war, an accident, an act of violence. But
it could also mean the end is finally coming to a long era
of suffering.

Reversed: The suffering has ended. Things look optimistic
or promising. Counsel and prayer help to ease in the new
transition. Things can only get better.

PAGE OF SWORDS

PAGE OF SWORDS

A YOUNG PAGE COVERED IN MAIL GRASPS HIS sword with two hands. It is heavy and he is still learning how to use it, as opposed to the knight of his suit who can wield the sword in one hand. Dark clouds that gather in the night sky behind him suggest trouble brewing. In the background, a young tree has sprung up out of a crevice and thrived.

Meaning: A youth attracted to the military. Possibility of an unstable home life or streak of inborn instability. Observant and interested in being of service. A spy. Quiet, but ignores nothing. May attend a military academy or some sort of training school. Eager to leave the school or home environment. A discontented youth.

Reversed: Reform school. Mandatory counseling. A troublemaker. Impostor revealed. Will do anything to belong. A threat to safety. Creates trouble that involves everybody. Bad companion. Bad influence. Sneaky.

KNIGHT OF SWORDS

KNIGHT OF SWORDS

A STERN-FACED KNIGHT FLIES IN ON AN ANGRY but beautiful horse. His sword is upraised; he expects trouble and creates trouble wherever he goes. He and his horse wear beautiful colors and attractive garments. The knight makes a grand entrance and has magnetic appeal; however, the swift moving-storm clouds suggest trouble.

Meaning: A warrior type, swift and aggressive. For a woman, a man will appear out of nowhere and a relationship will quickly begin. Fast-moving, quick-thinking, decisive young person already out forging their way in the world. Analytical and swift to action. A take-charge type of person that quickly defeats his opponents. Quick to love, quick to anger. He can create change for the better or worse. Self-confident and aggressive. Creates conflicts when aggravated.

Reversed: Someone disappears quickly and without much warning. Extravagance. Over-inflated ego. Jealous, violent temper. A person who needs to be restrained from dangerous actions.

QUEEN OF SWORDS

QUEEN OF SWORDS

A BRAVE, SOLEMN, BEAUTIFUL QUEEN CAPABLY holds forth the sword of her suit. Her hand grasps it tightly as if she is on constant alert and defense. She wears protective mail and armor but a flowing, silky violet sheath covers it. She stands over a forest at night. Icy mountains cast a silver glow under storm clouds. The double-edged sword indicates she has the quick intelligence to cut through both sides of a matter to arrive at fair decisions.

Meaning: A woman touched by sadness over the loss of a loved one. She could be a widow or divorced, anyone who has suffered a loss and is left to fend for herself and those she loves. She is strong, capable, stern, a force to be reckoned with in the business world or field of law. She is protective of herself and those she loves. This tough exterior does not mean she is incapable of emotion. She is capable of deep passion but does not give her heart easily. There is a light around her and despite her protective shell, she attracts men like a magnet.

Reversed: A bitter and spiteful woman who maligns and casts shadows of doubt on the character of anyone who irritates her. Imagined slights. Nervous, neurotic behavior. One who wraps themselves up in an exhausting whirlwind of activity, dancing, gymnastics, socializing, working, mindless fun—anything to suppress deep sadness. Fear of being overtaken by depression.

KING OF SWORDS

KING OF SWORDS

THE KING OF SWORDS IS DEFIANT AND SERIOUS with his sword up, ready to defend. His cape appears steel-like, yet it is in a constant state of motion. His aggression and intellect are finely tuned. His proud bearing and strong, mail-gloved hand indicate he has won many battles to get where he is and he intends to defend his throne. Steep green mountains reach up to a black sky. Storm clouds seem to be parting to allow light from above to shine through.

Meaning: A man with many hard-won achievements and accomplishments. An expert in law, military, and government. Proven leadership ability and position of authority. Matter-of-fact and to-the-point, practical advice. Possessive and protective of what is his own and what or who he believes to be his. Tendency toward harsh, quick judgements, but not closed-minded or unreasonable. Interested in keeping on top of skills and continually learning.

Reversed: Manipulative, dominating, aggressive, forceful, and uncaring. Evil person with an opportunistic character ready and waiting to take advantage. Seeks out the weak points in his opponents and jabs them before provoked. Jumps to conclusions without discerning facts, resulting in disastrous decisions. Prone to arguments and fights. Can be violent.

THE SUIT OF RODS

ACE OF RODS

ACE OF RODS

A HAND EMERGES FROM THE CLOUDS HOLDING forth a jeweled and flowering rod above a lake and mountains. The rod in full bloom symbolizes the beginning of new ideas, growth, and inspiration. Its appearance in the heavens indicates the attributes are a blessed gift. The white, fluffy clouds suggest purity of motive, and the silvery, sparkling lake indicates divine intervention.

Meaning: Birth. Energy, fertility, and growth. Original ideas. Inventions. Creations. The birth of a child. The beginning of an enterprise. Ideas conceived, patterns created. Masculine, aggressive, and bold. Assertiveness. Joy. New beginning. Inspiration.

Reversed: Projects, ideas canceled. Closing of ventures, businesses. Loss of direction. Impotence. Infertility. Plans scrapped. Barrenness. Emptiness. Leaving town.

TWO OF RODS

TWO OF RODS

AN INTELLIGENT-LOOKING YOUNG MAN STANDS on a balcony looking out over the sea. The two rods over his shoulder indicate that intellectually he has much to offer the world. His position in the enclosure indicates he has not left his home or institute of learning to put the ideas into action. He appears to be a well-dressed man of comfortable means.

Meaning: Education. Learning. Seeds of knowledge. Secure environment enables higher learning, study, adventure. Restlessness motivates the urge to travel, find new areas of expression. Fortunes, real estate, riches. Mature, strong personality. Opinionated. Tendency to dominate.

Reversed: Depression, sorrow. Wasted energy. Attention to mundane matters. Projects on hold. Lack of support. Monomania.

THREE OF RODS

THREE OF RODS

A LONE MAN STANDS ON THE SHORE WHILE A SHIP sails upon the sea. His green cape flows to the ground and seems to fix him in his spot. He appears to be ready but needs help from another source to get his ideas off the ground. His helmet and three rods accentuate the readiness for venturing out into the world and putting the plan into action. He looks out expectantly, as if waiting for someone.

Meaning: Help needed to launch an idea. Plans are made, all operatives in position. Business travel. Productive meetings. A new venture is underway. Partnerships formed. Trade, barter, commerce. Applications.

Reversed: Disappointments. Usury. Being taken advantage of. Help offered that benefits only the one making the offer.

FOUR OF RODS

FOUR OF RODS

FOUR RODS ADORNED BY A FLOWERY WREATH MARK the entrance to a path that leads to a castle on a hill. The chain of roses adorning the poles symbolizes the union of desires. Dawn's sunlight appears over the mountain which suggests victory and rejoicing. This is the card of deserved success. The rewards of a bountiful home in a beautiful setting.

Meaning: Success. Real estate. Acquisitions. Celebrating victories, partnerships, marriages, alliances. Established home and financial life. Well-deserved success. Harmony. Romance. Good things for deserving people. Prosperity. Enjoy!

Reversed: Good things and good times, but on a smaller scale. Success, but less dramatic and without the feeling of self-reliance. Insecurities, adversaries on the horizon. A desire for more.

FIVE OF RODS

FIVE OF RODS

FIVE YOUTHS BATTLE IN THE BRUSH UNDER A crescent moon. The different garments indicate the various social classes and degrees of competence. They all appear to be holding their own in this competitive environment. All the rods bear growth which indicates worthy opponents.

Meaning: Competition and struggle. Anxiety in the relentless pursuit of wealth. Keeping up with the ever-changing field. Challenges. Tension and conflict in business. Differing opinions and strategies cause arguments. Tempers flare. Fights break out. Struggle for victory, dominance.

Reversed: Glitches in business deals, contracts. Straightening out minor problems before they escalate into major ones. Exercise, games, game plans. Recreation. Long talks, conversations, lectures.

SIX OF RODS

SIX OF RODS

A HORSEMAN IN A SUIT OF MAIL CARRIES A VICTORY wreath upon his rod. The decorated horse and upright rods are reminiscent of a victory parade. The rider looks proud, his body tilts slightly forward. The horse steps lively and a horn on his shield suggests the unique spirit of the mythical unicorn. The amethyst on the horseman's shoulder symbolizes intelligence and communication.

Meaning: Victory after a struggle. Triumph. Good news. Winnings. Diplomacy. To the victor goes the spoils. Intelligence and fortitude won the battle. Gain of wealth, position, and prestige. Success in challenges. An excellent negotiator.

Reversed: Fear. Win without gain. False pride. Arrogance. Humbling losses. Humility. Pyrrhic victory.

SEVEN OF RODS

SEVEN OF RODS

AN ASTUTE-FACED MAN WEARING AN ELABORATE helmet uses his rod to fend off six competing rods. His helmet and robe resemble the man waiting to launch a venture in the Three of Rods. However, his helmet is now feathered and he wears a gold neck band, so we know that he has not only launched his project, but tasted success. He aims to keep his position on top.

Meaning: Diligent, courageous effort to stay on top in one's field. The competition is unrelenting. Mental and physical force is necessary. The struggle to keep the wolves at bay. Holding one's own to keep a position of power. Maintaining control.

Reversed: Slipping in position. Losing power and influence. Embarrassment. Weakness. Failure to fight for oneself and dependents. Losing face. Letting everybody down, including yourself.

EIGHT OF RODS

EIGHT OF RODS

EIGHT FLOWERING RODS FLY THROUGH THE NIGHT from right to left. Their flight through the air indicates great speed and travel. Flowering rods symbolize growing intelligence and beauty. The stars twinkling in the background offer hope and insight from above. Quick communications, the speed of messages, swift travel and, since the rods appear to be landing, rapid approach to the goal.

Meaning: Plans go into action immediately. Air travel. Fast planes, trains, boats, and vehicles. Speed and accuracy. Electronic mail, faxes, messages. Instant access. Instant gratification. Pleasure. Good news. Safe landings. Thought transference. Excellent communication. Cupid's arrows of love. Vacations. Chance encounters of significance.

Reversed: Cancellation of plans. Delays. Arguments. Miscommunications. Things get lost in transit. Messages are misinterpreted. Displeasure. Jealousy.

NINE OF RODS

NINE OF RODS

A MAN WITH AN ALERT YET PLEASANT EXPRESSION holds a rod while eight other rods stand tall behind him. He has quite a few feathers in his cap, three small ones in front and two large ones on the side. Feathers indicate thought, aspirations, and successes. He seems comfortable in the position of defense which suggests he has fought and won before. He knows what to expect and is prepared.

Meaning: Capable defense of one's position. Attainment of goals. Success in one's field. Taking good care of self and others in your environment. Readying to meet challenges. Defense system in place. Good health. Preparedness.

Reversed: Defenses down. Injuries. Losing a battle. Abandonment. Fatigue. Loss of interest.

TEN OF RODS

TEN OF RODS

A WEARY TRAVELER TRUDGES ONWARD, DESPITE the strain of carrying ten heavy rods. The gray mountains and leafless trees indicate winter, a time of endings, and completion of a cycle. There is a weariness and sad determination to this person, as if the task is not satisfying on any level, but must be completed. He bears the burden alone with no sign of help anywhere.

Meaning: Strain from overbearing pressures, external or internal. Oppression. Determination to meet demands and complete tasks and projects. No rewards in sight. Time to finish the job and recover from the strain. Overburdened, but the task must be done. Feeling old and tired.

Reversed: Unbearable situation has ended. Completion of tasks. Release from tension. Closure. Time to leave the past behind.

PAGE OF RODS

PAGE OF RODS

A YOUNG EGYPTIAN PAGE STANDS ON A HILL ABOVE three pyramids in the desert. His decorated rod indicates association with nobility. Clouds gather, obscuring the future.

Meaning: A youth who touches all he meets with innocent yet profound messages of wisdom and hope. Intelligent, creative. Lover of the outdoors and nature. Musical, creative, inquisitive. May leave home early. Important messages. Spiritual person.

Reversed: Bad news, rumors, illness. Abrupt change of plans. Losing touch or communication with someone you value.

KNIGHT OF RODS

KNIGHT OF RODS

A KNIGHT RIDES A BEAUTIFUL WHITE HORSE WITH A flowing mane. His helmet has a scarlet plume, his flowering rod points to the future. Horses symbolize freedom and passionate sexuality. The forward-moving, colorful, and upbeat image suggests a magnetic personality full of ideas, great self-expression, and a restless, assertive nature.

Meaning: Irrepressible, forward-moving young person. Enthusiastic, interesting person not ready to settle down. Travels, explorations, intellectual pursuits. Good-natured and flirtatious. Fiery personality, quick to passion, quick to burn out. The coming or going of matters. Departures and absences. A person out in the world trying to get ahead. This person enjoys playing the field and is not ready to settle down.

Reversed: Jealousy and discord. Unstable relationship. Restless. Unable to create ties. Succumbing to temptations regardless of outcome.

QUEEN OF RODS

QUEEN OF RODS

THE QUEEN OF RODS IS ATTRACTIVE WITH A serious expression and enchanting green eyes. She holds a beautiful rod as a scepter. It blossoms forth a glowing white flower. Branches grow and curl and she holds another white flower in her hand. The rod bears a jewel similar to those in her crown. She stands, draped in ermine-trimmed robes in tall grasses by a mountain in the night.

Meaning: A woman who is fond of the countryside and nature. She is intelligent, expressive, lively, and magnetic; fond of home life, family, and friends. She is inspired, assertive, and willing to help others, especially children. She has a warm and direct sexual nature and usually marries and has a house filled with children and animals. Self-expression is important to her.

Reversed: Jealous and insecure. Mundane thoughts and aspirations. Economical to the point of being ridiculous. Dominating. Unfaithful.

KING OF RODS

KING OF RODS

A HANDSOME KING WITH FINE FEATURES HOLDS A jeweled and flowering rod. He stands on a balcony decorated with the flames of fire associated with his suit. He wears a jeweled crown and epaulet, and an ermine-trimmed cape similar to the Queen of Rods. A roaring, charging lion symbolic of his sun sign Leo is on his sleeve. A steep mountaintop glows from the light of the full moon.

Meaning: Energetic, passionate man of high ideals and principles. Attracted to nature, agriculture, and the country. He generally marries and has children. He finds comfort in home life but is very aggressive and can be hot-tempered in the outside world. Fond of animals, sciences, philosophy. Finds relaxation outside of the city. Stubborn and willful.

Reversed: Arrogant, hot-headed person. Unfaithful. Deceptive business practices. Obsessed with self. Pipe dreams.

THE SUIT OF CUPS

ACE OF CUPS

ACE OF CUPS

A HAND FROM A CLOUD PRESENTS A GOLDEN chalice overflowing with the stream of Paradise and raining the drops of Yod over the earth. A white dove, symbol of the exalted state of spirituality, carries the Holy Eucharist, the Christian symbol of the body of Christ, son of God. The equal-sided cross represents the union of positive and negative, heaven to earth. Lotus flowers in the bud stage and full blossom of life float upon the water. Lotus flowers symbolize the microcosm within the macrocosm.

Meaning: Great love. New beginnings. Emotional happiness. Births. Feminine influence. Love affairs, engagements, marriages. Reciprocal love. A very lucky, positive card promising emotional fulfillment. Devotion. True friendships. Spiritual enlightenment.

Reversed: Love dissipates. Unrequited love. Loneliness. Parting of lovers. Emotional sorrow and unhappiness. Endings. Regrets.

TWO OF CUPS

TWO OF CUPS

A MAN AND WOMAN HOLD THEIR CUPS TOWARD each other in a toast. Their eyes meet, conveying a look of mutual trust, respect, and understanding. They both wear similar wreaths symbolizing the joining of opposites in a victorious celebration. Overhead a winged lion's head appears over a staff upon which two snakes entwine. The lion represents the animal nature, the wings holy origin. The snakes entwine to symbolize a pact or joint agreement. Together the image implies the union was heaven blessed, a fateful partnership.

Meaning: Marriage and partnerships. Mutual love, admiration, and trust. Contracts. Agreements. Prenuptial agreements. Written understanding. Emotional affinity. Meeting of the minds. Joint ventures.

Reversed: Divorce. Separation. Broken contracts. Disharmony. Jealousy. Vindictive behavior. Harmful gossip. Bitterness.

THREE OF CUPS

THREE OF CUPS

THREE WOMEN LOOK FORWARD IN STRIPED flowing robes that seem to swirl and move in graceful fluidity. Blossoming, violet-colored flowers and thistles adorn the base of the card. Their cups are adorned with amethyst jewels. They appear as the Three Graces who celebrate harmony, peace, and abundance.

Meaning: Rejoice! A cause of celebration. Success, abundance, prosperity. Joyous ceremonies and events. A time of happiness and plenty. Marriages, births, healings. Community celebrations. Happy social gatherings. A season of pleasure.

Reversed: Over-indulgence. Taking advantage of people. Inebriation. Excess. Wanton behavior. Promiscuity. Wild abandon. Unbridled passion. Lack of self-control. Guilt. Aftermath.

FOUR OF CUPS

FOUR OF CUPS

A YOUNG MAN HAS RETREATED TO THE MEADOW TO sit under a tree ripe with fruit. He studies four cups before him, but makes no effort to reach for them.

Meaning: Ambivalence toward that which has been offered. Advice and opportunities offered from friends and family, none of which have great appeal. Comfortable in current position, yet yearning for something more. Satisfied, yet bored. Stationary. Sameness. Inexplicable moodiness. Complacency. Temporary period of self-absorption and introversion. Reflection.

Reversed: Movement toward improvements. Venturing out in the world to make new acquaintances and broaden one's horizons. New friendships. Premonitions. Doors open. Renewed appreciation of family and friends. Gloominess lifts. Self-improvement.

FIVE OF CUPS

FIVE OF CUPS

A HAUNTING IMAGE OF A DEPRESSED MAN ALONE ON a plateau of leafless, craggy brush. He seems to be mourning a loss or something out of reach, perhaps something in the castle on the hill. He looks down at the spilled cups scattered before him, yet turns his back on the two full cups.

Meaning: Something was lost, but something is left. Failure to work with the positive due to concentrating on the negative. Disillusioned, perhaps overreacting to a disappointment. Depression. Hurt feelings. Loss of friend or loved one. Divisions that seem irreparable. Sadness, regrets. Betrayal. Let down by a friend or loved one. Unhappy relationship.

Reversed: Reappearance of an old friend or loved one. Unexpected reunion. Emotional healing after deep disappointment. Second chances. Movement. Returning to the rhythm of life.

SIX OF CUPS

SIX OF CUPS

A REASSURING CARD OF CUPS OVERFLOWING WITH beautiful flowering plants and foliage. The wind blows the grass in the background suggesting movement of time. The colors and good feelings and memories derived from the stationary cups will last forever.

Meaning: Happy memories in the making. Unconditional love and pleasure from children, friends, and family. Playfulness. Beauty. Precious moments that will exist in the mind forever. Love and care of family that repeats generation to generation. Emotional security. Stable, healthy home and family environment. The past is linked to the future.

Reversed: Returning to familiar ways of the past when overwhelmed by challenges. Immaturity. Naiveté. Unhappy childhood. Regression. Therapy and counseling. Living in the past hampers future growth.

SEVEN OF CUPS

SEVEN OF CUPS

SEVEN CUPS AGAINST A PURE, WHITE BACKGROUND, each holding a colorful image which suggests a creative and imaginative mind with many avenues from which to choose. Cascading flowers suggest a beautiful but short life span which must be lived to the fullest each day; the rainbow represents hope with rewards; the sun denotes power, energy, intelligence; the crescent moon indicates mental reflection, psychic powers, and intuition; the serpent speaks of secret wisdom; the fire ignites passion; and the water holds thought.

Meaning: A creative intelligence that can excel in more than one field. Deep interest in many subjects. A wonderful combination of talents that need the right environment all through life for proper attunement and expression. A unique, multi-talented personality. Marvelous ideas. Inspirational person.

Reversed: Scattered energies. Wasted talents. Frustration. Self-expression hindered. Repressed emotions emerge in unproductive, sometimes dangerous ways. Failure to find true expression. Schizophrenic behavior. Time to choose one of many talents to develop or find a way to combine them all.

EIGHT OF CUPS

EIGHT OF CUPS

THERE IS A LOT OF MOVEMENT AND ACTIVITY coming from the elemental forces. The ground and mountains appear in a state of transition. The smoky clouds billow softly then gather momentum and burst upward. The moon is full and lights up the landscape as if it were day. A man, with garments and a walking stick similar to a hermit's, walks away from eight full cups.

Meaning: Compulsion to leave an established situation to seek something higher. An inner drive forces one to abandon a comfortable situation. Outgrowing a situation or relationship. A good time to leave. The quest or search for new meaning in life. The realization that life is rushing past and now is the time to activate your desires.

Reversed: Abandoning a good relationship for foolish reasons. Always wondering what could have been. Return from mental or physical abandonment. The prodigal son returns. The wayward lover comes home.

NINE OF CUPS

NINE OF CUPS

A GOOD-NATURED, CHUBBY, GRAYING MAN EYES THE feast on the table. Nine cups are stacked neatly on a stepped pyramid shape behind him. A pomegranate split open reveals seeds of productivity and regeneration. Fish from the sea and fruit from the tropics suggest this man has traveled extensively and enjoyed life to the fullest.

Meaning: Goodwill and generosity. A life well lived. A good-natured person with lots of experience and warmth. A welcome environment with plenty of food and drink. Good fortune, material and physical well-being. Comfortable environment with everything in abundance.

Reversed: People take advantage of good-natured generosity and willingness to help. Ill health from overindulgence. Lack of judgement. Emotional addictions. Untrustworthy person in the midst. Weak-willed, too easygoing.

TEN OF CUPS

TEN OF CUPS

A RAINBOW OF TEN CUPS ARCHES OVER A PEACEFUL river and lush green landscape. A tower sits on a distant hill. Blue sky and fluffy clouds surround the rainbow's light. Rainbows symbolize hope, wishes coming true, and finding one's "pot of gold" after a long search. They are beautiful things of nature that seem to magically appear after storms when the sun is first breaking through.

Meaning: A wonderful marriage, a secure and happy home. True happiness and emotional contentment. Weddings. True friendship. Proven friendships that have survived and flourished in good times and bad. Complete contentment and attainment of emotional well-being. High self-esteem and popularity.

Reversed: Troubled home. A quarrel between family members. Engagements are off, marriage partners separate or live in bitterness. Sorrow and loss of peace within the family. Betrayal by friends. Loss of home. Uncomfortable family and extended family relationships.

PAGE OF CUPS

PAGE OF CUPS

A YOUNG PERSON GAZES AT A FISH EMERGING FROM a cup. The large hat symbolizes meditation, and the feather, contemplation. The tassels that resemble the cap of the jester recall the Fool's easygoing nature and open mind. The fish represents ideas surging up from the deep subconscious to find expression on the earthly plane.

Meaning: Creative intelligence and artistic talent. A sensitive youth who loves the home and family is a good and faithful friend. Imaginative, emotionally expressive, gentle, and interested in other people's feelings. A meditative person willing to please and be helpful.

Reversed: Easily hurt. Prone to tears. Needs to develop a tough veneer to survive. "Wishy-washy." Dependent. Embellishes and fabricates stories and gossip.

KNIGHT OF CUPS

KNIGHT OF CUPS

A KNIGHT IN ARMOR WITH A MAGENTA PLUME HOLDS up a jeweled cup. He seems to be contemplating it as if to try to understand the meaning of his suit, the world, and his place in it. Thistles bloom and grow on a vine beside him. Purple mountains with jagged peaks are off in the distance. His soft eyes and slender hands paint a picture of a soft, sensitive person. The wings on his helmet are reminiscent of Mercury who brings messages and invitations.

Meaning: An enthusiastic, open-minded, artistic, romantic person. Sensitive and perceptive to the feelings and moods of the times and people around him. May seem effeminate if male, sensual and sexually open-minded. Love of travel. Very sociable, agreeable, chatty. Proposals and propositions. An invitation. A gift.

Reversed: Promiscuous. Witty and entertaining but jealous and nasty. Tendency toward excess. Escapist tendencies. May have trouble with weight, alcohol, or drugs.

QUEEN OF CUPS

QUEEN OF CUPS

AN ENCHANTING QUEEN DRAPED IN AZURE, THE color of tranquillity, which evokes thoughts of clear skies and translucent waters, closes her eyes and wears a mysterious Mona Lisa-like smile. The cup before her is filled, and her crown is adorned with many jewels. Her robe gently surrounds with the fluidity of a wave coming up from the sea.

Meaning: An emotional and kindly woman, sensitive to beauty and nature. Happiest and inspired when around water. Romantic and interested in the arts: literature, fine arts, crafts, drama, music, ballet. Passionate and sensitive, motivated by compassion and a desire to nurture. Attractive female with expressive eyes and gentle nature. Sensual and erotic. Loyal and helpful to family; eternally attractive as a mate.

Reversed: Irrational and jealous. Controlled by insecurity. Emotional neediness exhausts herself and others. Imaginary fears, aches, and illnesses. Constant worrier. Propelled by desire to seduce and to be loved and adored, which can lead to unfaithfulness and the ruin of those involved.

KING OF CUPS

KING OF CUPS

A KING, REGALLY ATTIRED AND BEJEWELED, HOLDS a cup and scepter. In the distance, a ship sails and a dolphin leaps from the sea. His eyes are as blue as the ocean, and despite the air of authority and importance his attire evokes, his features reveal a softness that indicates intuition and sensitivity. The ship suggests commerce and trade. The dolphin represents deep intelligence, excellent communication, thoughts springing forth from the deep.

Meaning: An authoritative but compassionate man who is a leader. Artistic, creative with deep understanding and vision. Performs duties with ease and imagination. He is secretive, passionate, and offers no explanations, which tends to frustrate those around him. Ambitious, authoritative, and manipulative. Self-absorbed, he can seem lost in his thoughts but then creates spectacular feats and excels in his field. Attracted to and inspired by the sea, lakes, and rivers. Passionate and secretive, he is generous to those he loves.

Reversed: An unjust, evil man with a violent temper. Destroys those who cross him or get in his way. Manipulative and cold.

THE SUIT OF PENTACLES

ACE OF PENTACLES

ACE OF PENTACLES

A HAND FROM THE HEAVENS EMERGES FROM A billowing cloud. It holds a jeweled pentacle over the earth. The river symbolizes the continuity of life and the subconscious, and the rounded, orbed ground, the physical earth. There is a strong three-dimensional feel to this card, particularly in the way the clouds part yet encircle the pentacle. The talent and ability to reap material gain on earth is a gift from the Divine.

Meaning: The beginning of great wealth. A generous inheritance. Success in financial matters. New employment. Monetary gains. Blessed by material comforts. Successful projects and ventures. An excellent omen.

Reversed: Monetary losses. Financial ruin. Loss of employment. Missed opportunity. Fear of success.

TWO OF PENTACLES

TWO OF PENTACLES

A YOUNG MAN MAINTAINS A PLEASANT, ALERT outlook as the pentacles balance back and forth in the symbol of the harmonious universe. Finance and projects are difficult to develop; however, the budding plant in the foreground promises things will blossom soon.

Meaning: Harmony during change. Juggling finances. Money goes up and down. Change of employment. Launching a new business. Success is in the future, keeping the ship afloat is of concern now.

Reversed: Unbalanced accounts. Loss of income. Temporary setbacks. Anxiety about money and position.

THREE OF PENTACLES

THREE OF PENTACLES

A CRAFTSMAN WORKS WITH HAMMER AND CHISEL while gazing at the landscape and future ahead. The intricacy of his craftwork reveals exacting talents. He appears to be working in a church which would involve meetings, plans, contracts, and obligations. He is near completion of the archway and looks out into the landscape for inspiration and contemplation of future projects. A career is underway.

Meaning: Skilled labor or craft. Specialized training ensures future success. Enjoyable employment. Apprenticeship. Talent. Architecturally inclined. Creating designs for building. Study. Working diligently. Self-improvement. Refining and sharpening skills. Confidence develops through pride in work.

Reversed: Too many irons in the fire. Impossible to succeed when energies are scattered. Undeveloped skills. Unskilled labor. Costly mistakes. Unsatisfying work. Too little effort. Dissatisfaction with course of study and/or career choice.

FOUR OF PENTACLES

FOUR OF PENTACLES

A KING SITS ON A THRONE HOLDING PENTACLES under two fruit-bearing trees. The fruit represents the rewards of his efforts. The trees are projects he carefully tended and cultivated and now are practically running themselves. The grasping manner in which he holds the pentacles reveals a possessive nature. He wants to hold on to what he worked hard to achieve. The pentacle over his head shows money is on his mind.

Meaning: Success and security. Obsession with monetary gain subdues other interests. Frugality. Possessive person. Fear of letting go. Accumulation of riches. Miser.

Reversed: Expenditures exceed income. Many bills come at once. Funds depleted. Investment losses. Expensive repairs and unexpected bills. Anxiety due to monetary losses.

FIVE OF PENTACLES

FIVE OF PENTACLES

AN UNFORTUNATE COUPLE WEIGHED DOWN BY THE strains of penury and ill health huddle past the church on a snowy, black night. The pale faces and cold, white snow amplify the contrast of warmth and light shining from inside the church. They suffer the depths of poverty and despair.

Meaning: Poverty. Misery. Ill health. Nowhere to turn. Mental and physical strain due to financial hardships. Loss of home and income. Loss of physical comfort and companionship. Lovers torn apart.

Reversed: Poverty lifts, albeit slowly. Lovers find ways to meet. Relationships repaired. Recovery and healing. Spiritual guidance.

Six of Pentacles

SIX OF PENTACLES

SCALES SUSPENDED IN A STARRY NIGHT HOLD perfectly balanced coins. The position of the scales in the heavens over earth implies financial success generated on earth is a direct result of being blessed with special talent; therefore, the rewards should be used to help others less fortunate.

Meaning: Inspiration to help others financially. Charity. Endowments. Support of the arts and other worthy causes. Balanced accounts. Enough financial security to be free to help others. Donations to causes of interest. Generosity.

Reversed: Money used to manipulate and coerce. Wasteful expenditures. Bad investments.

SEVEN OF PENTACLES

SEVEN OF PENTACLES

A WELL-DRESSED, SERIOUS-LOOKING MAN CONTEMplates a growing tree that is full of pentacles. The walking staff indicates he has come a long way with his ideas and carefully monitors their growth. His concerned gaze at the full-grown tree suggests his efforts are at a point where they should be rewarding him; however, they still cling to the tree.

Meaning: Cultivation and careful attention to a project that promises to bring success. Great effort expended, now to realize the gain. Careful financial planning and monitoring business interests. Tricky financial situation. Waiting to collect money owed.

Reversed: Anxiety and problems with loans or past investments. Unfruitful ventures. Possible rejection of loan. Loans from unconventional sources. Need for additional income to survive while tending a greater interest.

EIGHT OF PENTACLES

EIGHT OF PENTACLES

A CRAFTSMAN INTENT ON HIS CREATION SITS ON A workbench with his past credentials above him. His intent gaze shows genuine interest in his work. His relaxed posture indicates confidence and experience. He is a virtuoso in his craft.

Meaning: Creativity and success in one's chosen field. Past successes. Financial and emotional success. Excellence in a profession. Skilled labor. Talented person. Capable and dependable. Detail-oriented. A career well under way.

Reversed: Loss of interest in profession causes sloppy work that leads to other problems. Second-rate work. Commercialism. Staleness in the workplace.

NINE OF PENTACLES

NINE OF PENTACLES

A WELL-DRESSED WOMAN GAZES AT AN EXOTIC BIRD perched on her caped shoulder. The cape is a symbol of self-protection, but also of isolation. She is surrounded by luxury and beautiful things and enjoys them alone. Grapes which symbolize cultivation and abundance grow in the foreground and promise continued success.

Meaning: Attainment of goals. Abundance. Comfort and luxury. Independent means. Good fortune. Love of beautiful things. Good taste. Love of travel and acquiring things from exotic and exciting locations. Refined and cultured person.

Reversed: Protect assets. Be careful with investments. Beware of swindlers. Naiveté invites the unscrupulous to take advantage.

Ten of Pentacles

TEN OF PENTACLES

A MAN PROTECTIVELY ESCORTS HIS WIFE BENEATH a columned archway to their castle on the hill. The symmetry and balance of the columns and towers are reflective of the same attributes in the couple. The substantial home and solidity of materials in the home and archway show that wealth and success are here to stay and will be passed on to future generations.

Meaning: High achievements and satisfaction on the earthly plane. Wealth and security passed down from generation to generation. Completion of work. Rewards enjoyed. Estates and dynasties. Great success and the advantages it brings. Excellent real estate holdings and profitable investments.

Reversed: Great fortunes lost. A wealthy home, but one which is troubled by family problems. Dysfunctional family. Public embarrassments stemming from wayward or talkative family members. Negative press.

PAGE OF PENTACLES

PAGE OF PENTACLES

AN ELEGANTLY-DRESSED YOUTH HOLDS OUT HIS hand and a pentacle seems to magically draw near. His closed eyes indicate the ease with which he attains it. The feather in his hat indicates intelligence and faith. A soft smile reveals a sensual nature.

Meaning: The Page of Pentacles represents a cultivated and refined youth of high ideals. He is serious, scholarly, and will choose a road that develops his interests and allows him to appreciate the finer things in life. He or she has a scientific, analytical mind. A physical, sensual person.

Reversed: Careless, illogical, and selfish. Pampered, immature, and unable to comprehend the give and take in any sort of relationship, be it in friendship, love, or academic or work environment.

KNIGHT OF PENTACLES

KNIGHT OF PENTACLES

AN ARMORED KNIGHT RIDES A SOLID-LOOKING black workhorse. In his mailed gloved hand he holds a pentacle upon which he focuses his attention. Plumed feathers burst out from his helmet. Green hills and trees in the background echo the connection to the earth and the physical nature of his suit. Slow and steady like the workhorse, he diligently and laboriously pursues the pentacles.

Meaning: A capable and dependable person. Well-trained and educated. Opinionated. Interested in science and culture. Methodical. Hard-working person. Zest for one's chosen career path. Diligent and helpful. A good mind. Can be a workaholic. Physically fit. Sexually conservative and loyal.

Reversed: Narrow-minded. Dull. Plods along producing mediocre work. Indolent. Gossipy. Snide. Lazy. Critical.

QUEEN OF PENTACLES

QUEEN OF PENTACLES

A STARRY NIGHT ILLUMINATES THE STRIKING silhouette of the Queen of Pentacles. The pentacle appears in her thoughts with a round blue jeweled center. Stylized plants of her earth sign line the base. She has the innate attraction to the material as does her sun sign, Capricorn.

Meaning: The Queen of Pentacles represents a cultured, refined, and wealthy woman who is a patron of the arts and charities. She is intelligent and practical, willing to work hard and lobby for the support of her interests. Able to generate wealth, warmth, and comfort. A secure person, quick to realize the potential in others. Loyal and supportive of family and friends. Sociable, physical, sensual.

Reversed: Materialistic and prone to complaining. Unwilling to help others. Self-centered and disagreeable. Suspicious of everybody. Narrow-minded. Actively seeking out the worst in people.

KING OF PENTACLES

KING OF PENTACLES

A STARRY BLACK NIGHT ALSO ILLUMINATES THE silhouette of the King of Pentacles. He faces the queen of his suit. Two trees and a field of waving grass in the background connect the pentacles' association with the earth. He has the determination and stubbornness of his sun sign, Taurus. The sky shines pure white behind him.

Meaning: Shrewdness, intelligence, and determination have made the King of Pentacles a wealthy man. Whether he earned his money from development, real estate, ranching, wine-making, or any other field connected to the earth or managed inherited wealth, he did so with great success. Willing to help others. Ability to analyze people quickly and capably. Loyalty to and from family. Physically active. Virile.

Reversed: "Earthy" with the tendency to be vulgar. Materialistic and greedy. Uncouth. Dull. Poor temperament. Attracted to wealth but unable to successfully generate an income. Excessive behavior. Gambler. Critical and lazy. Stingy. Unable to adapt to changing times. Hypocritical. Prejudiced and narrow-minded. Perversion. Selfish and unfaithful as a lover or husband.

READING TAROT CARDS

PREPARING TO READ

Atmosphere is everything when reading Tarot cards. It tunes in the reader and gets the querent to be in the right state of mind. The reader sits facing north with legs and arms uncrossed. Try to be in a quiet room, away from distractions. A lit candle or incense is wonderful for atmosphere but not necessary.

•◆•

THE QUERENT

The person who is having their cards read is sometimes referred to as the seeker, or querent. If you are reading for someone who is intellectually open, has had accurate readings in the past, or has predicted things themselves, then the reading will go fine. If you find yourself with someone who is too frivolous in their approach or is closed-minded, expect difficulties or decline to read. People who are closed-minded are negative and therefore can spoil an otherwise pleasurable, enlightening experience. One time, though, I found myself reading for a pessimistic elderly man. It was at a small social gathering and it would have been rude to exclude him. I was uncomfortable and resentful of his remarks such as "Oh, I'll have them read but I don't believe...blah blah." I quickly offered not to read his cards, but to my dismay he pulled up a chair. He amused himself with sarcasm all the way through the reading. A few months later he sent me a postcard saying that the reading was eerily accurate, particularly what had showed up about his father, and although he still wasn't a "convert" he wanted me to know he was now thinking there may be "something to it."

As a reader, you may find yourself favoring certain types of people. I particularly like to read for creative people, people in the arts, spiritual people, and people who do a lot of traveling.

• ◆ •

SHUFFLING

Shuffle the cards while concentrating on a question and don't stop until you feel ready. If you don't have a question, ask, "What do I need to know?" or "What will the next few months bring?"

If a card seems to "fly" out of the deck, read it. When this happens to me, the card invariably is relevant to my question! If it happens to someone you are reading for, memorize the card(s) that fell out and see if they reappear in the reading. If someone drops a lot of cards on the floor, they could be just nervous. Tell them to take their time and not worry about you.

• ◆ •

CARDS COLOR ONE ANOTHER

As an art major in college, one of my first projects was to paint a pure color square. Then, in a series of 20 or so one-inch cubes, we kept adding more and more white until we reached pure white. The process was repeated, only this time adding more and more black until reaching pure black. We did this with many colors. The next project was to put different colors beside each other and notice what happened. Blue and orange stripes seemed to vibrate, gray and lavender looked peaceful, and so on.

When Tarot cards land beside each other in a reading, they color the meanings in much the same way. For example, if the Three of Swords lands between the Nine of Swords and Ten of Rods, the broken heart will cause terrible pain, suffering, and angst. If the Three of Swords lands between the Six of Cups and Knight of Cups, the pain of a broken heart will be eased by caring friends.

• ◆ •

TIPS ON CARD READINGS

Major Arcana cards represent an important phase you are going through. If half of the spread is made up of Major Arcana cards, write it down. The reading will be of great value because it speaks of major life evolutions rather than just mundane events.

Court cards represent people. Kings represent men who are established in life, queens are women, knights can be males or females out in the world, pages can be males or females who are still living at home or in school. Knights and pages can also represent comings or goings of matters related to their suit.

Numbered trumps are activities, ideas, emotions, and material concerns.

If there are a lot of cups in a spread, the reading is describing emotional concerns, happiness, love, and marriage. A lot of pentacles point toward finances, work, business, and money matters. A lot of swords indicate aggression, trouble, and strife. A lot of rods suggest energy, intellect, and opposition.

If you notice a concentration of specific numbers or court cards, refer to the following list to determine the direction the reading will take:

4 Aces . . . . New beginnings in every phase of life, success, a powerful new start

3 Aces . . . . Excellent omen, good luck, fresh starts

4 Kings. . . . Swift conclusions to all matters, important news

3 Kings. . . . News regarding conflicts

4 Queens . . Great influence, important social events

3 Queens . . Powerful friends

4 Knights . . Past acquaintances

3 Knights . . Social invitations abound

4 Pages. . . . New plans

3 Pages. . . . Sociable youth

4 Tens. . . . . Great responsibility

3 Tens. . . . . Important business position

4 Nines. . . . Near completion

3 Nines. . . . Correspondence

4 Eights . . . News, gaiety

3 Eights . . . Journeys

4 Sevens . . . Good luck, contracts

3 Sevens . . . Disappointments

4 Sixes . . . . Pleasure

3 Sixes . . . . Gain

4 Fives . . . . Order

3 Fives . . . . Troubles

4 Fours. . . . Peace

3 Fours. . . . Industry

4 Threes . . . Determination

3 Threes . . . Deceit

4 Twos . . . . Conversations

3 Twos . . . . Reorganizations, recommendations

• ◆ •

THE CELTIC CROSS SPREAD

The Celtic Cross is very popular because it's easy to do and is a wonderful way to learn how to adapt the meaning of a Tarot card to the particular "house" in which it falls. A house is an area of concern. The ten houses of the Celtic Cross are numbered below.

Shuffle the cards and divide them into three piles with the left hand. Pick one pile and spread the cards into the shape of the Celtic Cross.

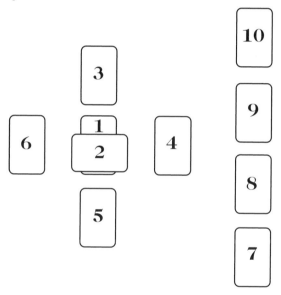

1. Subject
2. Crosses Subject
3. Past Events
4. Coming In or Going Out
5. Near Future

6. Within Weeks
7. Fears/Concerns
8. Family & Friends
9. Subconscious
10. Outcome

CELTIC CROSS SAMPLE READING

The querent is a 31-year-old single man named Nicholas. He shuffles the deck, thinking of a question. Two cards fly out. They are the Ten of Pentacles and the Knight of Swords, reversed: a high money card and an unstable knight. Nicholas said he was thinking of buying a very expensive gadget that has to be imported from another country. The Knight of Swords is reversed, which warns of quick, impulsive behavior. Since swords bring trouble, it seems an unwise purchase at this time. He should think about it for a few weeks. This incident is mentioned because it ended up tying in to the reading.

Nicholas reshuffles and asks, "What do I need to know?" He divides the cards into three piles and pushes one toward me to read. They are:

First, I glance at the total picture and note first impressions. The Eight of Cups reversed seems to be walking in the direction of the Six of Cups reversed, which represents the past. Nick is walking back into his past for something. The Fool is looking up at the Six of Cups, which indicates a pure motive. The Ace of Pentacles is beside the Fool, which suggests money matters. The Tower reversed and on its way out reveals a traumatic situation that has healed over time, but unresolved issues have resurfaced. The Emperor and two Kings lend an overall masculine feel to the reading; the situation in question involves many aggressive men. I read these impressions in a "stream of consciousness" fashion. There is an overall positive feel, except for the Five of Swords. A thief is around and Nick is already aware of this, but he doesn't comment yet.

The next step is to take a look at each card, finding ways they each interrelate to produce a cohesive reading.

1. The archetype active and present in Nick's life is the leadership and authority of the **Emperor.** He has to activate these qualities in himself and surround himself with other people like this for a particular battle, indicated by what crosses him.

2. He is crossed by the **Nine of Rods**—he is fighting for something and has already had a few victories but expects more trouble. The figure on the defense card is looking down at the King of Rods.

3. The **King of Rods** is someone from his past, someone from the countryside, maybe his father or grandfather. The impression is this father figure is connected to the struggle of defense Nick is involved in. At this point, Nick tells me he is indeed in a struggle; his father's family owned farmland in the country for seven generations.

His father died and left the land to him, his brothers, and a stepmother of a less-than-six-month marriage.

4. The traumatic event that happened a long time ago has resurfaced. The **Tower** in this position points to the devastation Nick felt when his dad passed away, and the messy state of affairs around the will.

5. The **Fool** in the near future indicates things are being prepared to be set in motion. This is Nick's first venture into a legal situation and he enters optimistically. The Fool being upright between the Emperor and Ace of Pentacles indicates he has everything on his side. Good counsel and good luck. A very good combination!

6. The **Six of Cups** when reversed can indicate a tendency to regress to old, familiar ways when overwhelmed. There are so many connections to the past in this case, I see this card as a warning to not get upset to the point of regressing into old bad habits, like drinking or getting depressed or anything like that. I don't know what Nick's particular bad habits are, so I can only warn him in this way. It is a family card, so he should be on the lookout for that tendency in his family members too. He said his bad regression could be the desire to go on wild shopping sprees, which is something he does when he's trying to cheer himself up. He then goes back and returns most everything the next day! Remember his first question? An impulsive, expensive purchase!

7. Nick's fears and concerns are represented by the **Five of Swords**—a thief! He says there is a thief; his stepmother has been taking timber off their land for years and his family has just found out. The land is substantial—almost 1,000 acres.

8. The **Ace of Pentacles** residing in the house of home and family is a very positive sign that things will work out in

his favor, and swiftly. It is a card of inheritance and material wealth.

9. The **King of Cups** reversed is in Nick's subconscious. He is harboring hateful feelings about the unfair treatment by his stepmother and he tends to obsess on them. He laughs and says that relates also to the "regressing to bad habits of old" warned of in the Six of Cups.

10. The final outcome, the **Eight of Cups**, is a return, which in context with the rest of the reading would indicate the land will return back to him and his brothers. His future is connected to the past. Also, he has an established career he enjoys, but has had to turn his back on it (compare to the person in the card turning their back on something established) to fight this land issue. It looks like he will be able to return to his career very soon.

The Emperor, the Fool, and the Ace of Pentacles are a very good combination for success.

•◆•

NINE-CARD EUROPEAN METHOD

My Lithuanian grandmother, Petra, taught me this reading. In the early 1900s, when she was 16, Petra was having tea at an outdoor cafe in Frankfurt, Germany. She said a "young gypsy man" who had cards with pictures on them kept bothering her and her girlfriends to let him tell their fortunes. They turned down his offer. However, before he left, he pulled out the cards and looked at my grandmother. He told her he would read her fortune anyway. He told her she would move to America, almost die the first year, marry a man who would be very successful but would break her heart, they would stay married, and she would have three sons. My grandmother blurted out she wanted daughters. The young gypsy smiled and shook his head. He told her she would be "surrounded by female grandchildren and would receive great joy from them." He also told she would have a huge garden. Everything he said came true. Regarding the garden, my grandfather purchased a baseball field adjacent to their property which my grandmother turned into the most beautiful garden with pebbled walkways, arbors, and a little fish pool. Petra told me this story when I was thirteen. I had never seen or heard of the Tarot prior to this; however, that same summer I bought my first deck.

This is the method the man used to so accurately read Petra's cards. Shuffle the cards, fan them out on a flat surface, and pick nine. The first three represent past events that shaped the present. The middle three represent the present. The last group represents the future.

•◆•

ASTROLOGICAL READINGS

Shuffle the cards and with your left hand separate them into three groups. Use the first pack that calls your attention.

Starting with the house of Aries, lay out the first twelve cards in a circle. You can reference the diagram in the book or draw out your own Zodiac Reading Map.

The twelve houses and what they represent are:

Aries ....Personality
Taurus..................Financial Affairs
Gemini.................Brothers, Sisters, Loves
Cancer ....Home Life
Leo.......................Love Affairs
Virgo ....Work
Libra ....Partnerships
Scorpio ....Sex, Birth, Death
Sagittarius.............Intellect
Capricorn ....Prestige, Possessions
Aquarius ....Social Activities, Groups
Pisces...................Emotions, Psyche, Karma

• ◆ •

ZODIAC READING
FOR THE YEAR AHEAD

You can also do a reading for the coming year using the same Zodiac Spread. The major happening of each month in a year can be read by what card lands on that sign's house. The houses are:

January	Capricorn
February	Aquarius
March	Pisces
April	Aries
May	Taurus
June	Gemini
July	Cancer
August	Leo
September	Virgo
October	Libra
November	Scorpio
December	Sagittarius

• ◆ •

TREE OF LIFE READING

This is the reading most useful in contemplating fate and destiny. Shuffle the cards, pull ten from the top and place in order by number over each correlating branch. Pull seven more cards and put them aside for later. This is called the "Daath" pack and will foretell the immediate future.

1. **Kether........crown**
   Highest intelligence
2. **Binah ....understanding**
   Life, "mother" card
3. **Chokmah ...wisdom**
   Creativity, "father" card
4. **Chesed ....mercy**
   Quest, force
5. **Geburah.....severity**
   Good qualities, virtues
6. **Tiphereth ...beauty - enlightenment**
   Health, spirit of sacrifice
7. **Netzach ......victory**
   Love, lust
8. **Hod............splendor**
   Procreation, arts
9. **Yesod ....foundation - psychic area**
   Imagination
10. **Malkuth .....kingdom - life on earth**
    Physical body, earthly home

Follow the diagram on page 214. The first triangle represents the spirit. The second triangle symbolizes the intellectual and moral nature. The third triangle denotes intuition and desires. Analyze the Tarot in relation to the house it falls on. Then meditate upon the combined meanings of cards within the triangles. When you're finished with the Tree of Life, read the Daath pack for the immediate future.

It is a good idea to keep a journal of readings to help build a better understanding of what you are reading, to look back and reaffirm what was interpreted and what came to pass. Intuition and perception increase with practice. Recording a reading allows you to check back and see if it was accurate. Perhaps it warned of something you didn't pick up at the time, but looking back you might see it was there in the cards.

Tree of Life

• ◆ •

TEA ROOM READINGS

USING THE WHOLE DECK

If you have ever gone into a "tea room" to have your cards read, you may have been asked to shuffle the cards and return them to the reader. The reader then takes each card and reads it one by one until the deck is finished. The reader is intuitively picking up something on each card that relates. For example, I had a reader do my cards in Boston and she turned over the Tower. What struck her was the floods. So, all she said was, "Your house—a flood." I knew what the card meant, so I figured she must have been picking out what first caught her eye. At the time, I was visiting my parents in Boston; however, I lived on the Russian River in Northern California, and the river did frequently overflow and get into our basement. We moved!

This type of reading is easy to do and wonderful to develop intuition, especially if you have a subject who offers feedback. Feedback can help you stay on track and zero in on the things important to the querent. If you read for yourself, it is hard to be objective, so flip over the cards, jot down what you noticed, and quickly move on the next. At the end, read down the list and keep it for reference.

21 CARDS

"Pick out 21 cards, then make a wish and take an extra card and put that card aside." You will hear this in tea rooms everywhere. I've had my cards read like this in the U.S., London, and Mexico. It seems this method is used frequently by people who read Tarot cards as a business.

The 21 cards are divided into three levels of seven. The top level is past, middle is present, bottom is future. The wish card will be answered positively or negatively.

•◆•

QUICK ANSWERS

Ask the question while shuffling. Cut the deck with your left hand and look at the last card in the top half. There is your answer.

•◆•

STORING THE CARDS

Keep the cards wrapped. I wrap mine in silk and store them in beautiful boxes I have collected for this purpose. This protects the cards and keeps the art of Tarot reading a special, serious occasion for contemplation and spiritual development.

•◆•

Good luck with your Tarot card readings and God Bless!

BIBLIOGRAPHY

Benavides, Rudolfo C. *The Prophetic Tarot.* Mexico: Editores Mexicanos Unidos, S.A. 1974.

Cavendish, Richard *The Tarot.* London: Michael Joseph, Ltd., 1975.

Cirlot, J.E.J. *A Dictionary of Symbols,* 2nd Edition, New York: Philosophical Library, 1972.

Crowley, Aleister. *The Book of Thoth (Egyptian Tarot),* New York: Samuel Weiser, Inc., 1969.

Douglas, Alfred. *The Tarot.* New York: Penguin Books, 1972.

Fortune, Dion. *The Mystical Qabalah.* New York: Alta Gaia Books, 1979.

Gerulskis-Estes, Susan. *The Book of Tarot.* Stamford, CT: U.S. Games Systems, 1981.

Gray, Eden. *A Complete Guide to the Tarot.* New York: Crown Publishers, 1970.

Gray, William G. *Inner Traditions of Magic.* New York: Samuel Weiser, 1970.

Hoeller, Stephan A. *The Royal Road: A Manual of Kabalistic Meditations on the Tarot.* Wheaton, IL: Theosophical Publishing House, 1975.

Jung, Carl G. *Man and His Symbols.* Garden City, NJ: Doubleday, 1964.

Kaplan, Stuart R. *The Encyclopedia of Tarot.* New York: U.S. Games Systems, 1978.

Kaplan, Stuart R. *The Encyclopedia of Tarot, Vol II.* Stamford, CT: U.S. Games Systems, 1986.

Kaplan, Stuart R. *The Encyclopedia of Tarot, Vol III*. Stamford, CT: U.S. Games Systems, 1990.

Levi, Eliphas. *The Key to the Myseries*. New York: Samuel Weiser, 1970.

Nichols, Sallie. *Jung and the Tarot*. York Beach, ME: Samuel Weiser, 1980.

Papus. *The Tarot of the Bohemians*, translated by A.P. Morton. 3rd edition. Los Angeles, CA: Wilshire Book Co., 1972.

Parrinder, Edward Geoffrey. *A Dictionary of Non-Christian Religions*. Philadelphia, PA: The Westminster Press, 1974.

Waite, Arthur Edward. *Pictorial Key to the Tarot*. Stamford, CT: U.S. Games Systems, Inc.